"If you're looking for a cushy, fluffy, make-me-feel-good-about-myself book, this is not the study for you. If, however, you yearn to grow deeper as a disciple of Jesus by learning what true spiritual maturity is and how to get there, this study of 1 Peter will help you mine each gem and do the hard work as Peter challenges us to do. Thank you so much for this resource, Amy!"

—Lynn Cowell, author of *Fearless Women of the Bible* and coauthor of *Esther: Seeing Our Invisible God in an Uncertain World*

"Reading *Can I Borrow a Cup of Hope?* is very much like having a trusted friend speak hope into the hardest places of your life. Amy is a gifted teacher, and her words are just the right mix of clever, funny, and profound. Each chapter offers biblical support and tangible steps to help us walk away from hopelessness and toward whatever God has planned."

—Peggy Bodde, founder of Sacred Work and author of *Sacred Work: Equipping Christian Women to Lead with Strength*

"*Can I Borrow a Cup of Hope?* is a beautiful, honest, and in-depth journey into 1 Peter that will leave you inspired, encouraged, and yes, even challenged, but in a good way. You'll come away a little humbler, a little more thoughtful and introspective, and best of all, a whole lot more able to set your hope fully on Christ, who has overcome all the trouble of this world."

—Jennifer Hayes Yates, author of *Just Like Us, Seek Him First*, and *Seeking Truth*

"I always considered *hope* one of the most dangerous words in the English language. Hope is a setup for heartbreak. Who needs that kind of pain? So when I got my hands on *Can I Borrow a Cup of Hope?*, I kept my expectations modest. Trust Amy to blow that attempt sky-high. Her humble and relatable voice blends story, rock-solid biblical teaching, and no-nonsense, practical wisdom in such a delightful way I was scarcely aware of my heart's crossover from 'nope' to 'hope.' I came away with a confidence in my loving Father I never knew possible."

—Leslie McLeod, blogger and artist

"Amy's study about hope came at God's perfect time. The world has been in a shutdown of fear and uncertainty about the future, but Amy's journey through 1 Peter reminds us of where our hope truly lies. Encouraging, challenging, and definitely worth reading."

—Sharon Jacobs, grateful gramma, harried homemaker, and blessed Neighborhood Café host

"Amy Lively's latest study, *Can I Borrow a Cup of Hope?*, invites each reader to engage in deep Bible learning while also remaining practical for every person's walk of faith. Each lesson is rich with historical context, honest application, and a challenging takeaway that will leave readers spiritually satisfied and anticipating the hope they will find in their hard places. Every reader will close this book with a Christ-centered approach to their hardships, as Lively makes the first-century letter of 1 Peter come to life for the twenty-first-century Christian."

—Bailey T. Hurley, author of *Together Is a Beautiful Place*

"This beautifully written, biblically rich deep dive into the life of Peter is a must-read. Full of scripture and real-life application, *Can I Borrow a Cup of Hope?* encourages readers to trade hopeless fears and hopeful fantasies for a firm and living hope found only in Jesus. Great for personal use or group study, this book is a resource you'll find yourself returning to again and again."

—Trinda Windle, ClearView Community Church women's ministry team

"If you're at the end of life as you know it, you need a cup of hope, and that's what Amy is serving. Like a neighbor who welcomes you in,

Amy masterfully blends words on the page—thoughtful lessons from 1 Peter—which will both comfort your soul and coax you into the saddle, ready for the trials ahead. You'll go from starting your sentences with, 'Hopefully . . .' to having your hope *fully* rooted in Jesus and all he has for you."

—Shannon Popkin, author of *Control Girl* and *Comparison Girl*

"I have known Amy Lively for many years, and I have got to say, this lady is the real thing. She doesn't just write about living with hope and loving your neighbor, she lives every word she writes. You'll see what I mean in *Can I Borrow a Cup of Hope?* Amy serves as a wise guide and companion on your journey to rediscover the hope that Jesus brings."

—Jennifer Rothschild, best-selling author and Bible study teacher

"In *Can I Borrow a Cup of Hope?* Amy Lively achieves two of my favorite things: engaging teaching and deep Bible study. This thoroughly researched study of 1 Peter weaves the scriptural threads of Peter's story together in ways that will challenge the mature Bible student and thrill the newest. As I connected my story to Peter's in the book's practical exercises, I had both 'aha' and 'oh ouch!' moments. This is the resource you need to fan the flame of hope."

—Amy Carroll, coauthor of *Esther: Seeing Our Invisible God in an Uncertain World*

"Suffering is something most people want to avoid, causing hopelessness and fear. But in reality, suffering is our privilege and a precious tool in the hands of our good, good Father, designed to conform us to the image of his Son, Jesus. Amy has taken deep truths about suffering and pointed us to the One who alone can provide all we need for any situation we face. Amy masterfully leaves us with grounding truth in one hand and a cup overflowing with hope in Jesus in the other."

—Debbie Dittrich, retreat speaker and Bible teacher

"Amy is that friend that encourages you and exhorts you in the same breath. She will pick you up, dust you off, and encourage you to keep running with fresh perspective on the very real and rooted hope we have in Christ. Far from defining hope as a pie-in-the-sky, saccharine wish, Amy shows us a hope that holds fast in stormy seas. She manages to define and defend hope (especially when things feel hopeless), while awakening the courage and the resolve of the Spirit within us and filling our cup for the next leg of the journey. I appreciated the invitation to dive deep at the end of each lesson, and her hands-on resources are a treasure. The problems we face are real, but we are not alone. Armed with engaging stories from the early church and from her own life, Amy invites us to remember together the grit from that great cloud of witnesses that came before and beckons us onward. Sure, we aren't home yet, but books like this and friends like Amy make the wait that much sweeter."

—Katie Zintek, speaker and women's ministry director at
Westwood Church, St. Cloud, MN

"With Amy's encouragement, turn your *hopefully*s into *hope fully* in the Lord. What a difference a space makes! Jesus tells us that in this world we will have trouble. How will I respond when trouble comes? This book challenges me once again that my conduct, especially during those times of trouble, speaks louder than words for my own personal relationship with God . . . and to those watching. This is a great resource for groups to do together."

—Lara Price, pastor at Life Church Vineyard, Pleasantville, OH

CAN I BORROW A CUP OF HOPE?

How to Find Faith for Hard Times in 1 Peter

AMY LIVELY

KREGEL
PUBLICATIONS

Can I Borrow a Cup of Hope?: How to Find Faith for Hard Times in 1 Peter
© 2023 by Amy Lively

Published by Kregel Publications, a division of Kregel Inc., 2450 Oak Industrial Dr. NE, Grand Rapids, MI 49505. www.kregel.com.

Cataloging-in-Publication data is available from the Library of Congress.

ISBN 978-0-8254-4785-3, print
ISBN 978-0-8254-7052-3, epub
ISBN 978-0-8254-6970-1, Kindle

Printed in the United States of America
23 24 25 26 27 28 29 30 31 32 / 5 4 3 2 1

To my daughter—
"O Emma, remember the Lord!"

Contents

~ ❊ ~

Begin Here

"WHERE ARE YOU TAKING ME?" a tiny voice from the middle row of the minivan demanded to know. Even as a toddler, our daughter noticed if we veered off our usual route. Emma knew her way around town and could tell us which way to turn to get to Mimi and Papa's house and which route to Grandma and Grandpa's might include a stop at her favorite playground.

I, on the other hand, am directionally challenged. Words like *east* and *northwest* are meaningless to me. I don't have an internal compass, and if it weren't for my car's navigation system, I would barely find my way to the grocery store.

But I do know where I want my life to go and how and when I expect to get there. The path for my career is carefully plotted, along with milestones for my retirement account. I've mapped out my ideal family. There will be some adorable grandchildren at the end of my trip as my husband and I grow old together, side by side in our rocking chairs overlooking the Rocky Mountains, or maybe under palm trees at the beach.

Oh, I know the Bible says God has perfectly good plans for me—but it also says his ways are not my ways. I happen to like my ways, thank you very much, and I spend a lot of time and effort making my careful plans. My plans are safe and easy, and I'm quite committed to them.

Now, you don't need me to tell you that life doesn't always go according to plan. Marriage is rarely easy. Your empty arms may ache to hold a child. Sickness can put you on the sidelines. Abuse and addiction weren't on your agenda, and you didn't schedule the day you'd be let go from your job or released from a relationship. These detours are more than traffic jams that make you late for work: they're BRIDGE OUT barricades that stop you in your tracks.

When I hit a dead end, brakes screeching and tires squealing, I remind God that this isn't what I had in mind when I booked this adventure. Like a little girl buckled up in the back seat for a bumpy ride, I cry out, "Where are you taking me?"

There's a name for this phenomenon when your hopes and dreams come to an abrupt dead end: TEOTWAWKI (pronounced tea-ot-wah-key). No, it's not a Greek or Hebrew word from the Bible; compared to these ancient languages, TEOTWAWKI is brand-new. This acronym has been in use for a few decades, and it stands for "The End of the World as We Know It."

Ever received a phone call that altered your entire world by the time you hung up? Have you sat through school conferences that enraged you or marriage counseling sessions that infuriated you? Me, too. I've answered the doorbell to find an IRS agent at my doorstep. I've taken a friend shopping for the outfit she would be buried in. I've raced to the accident scene, waited for the ambulance, done vigil in the hospital room, and held hands as the doctor delivered a devastating diagnosis and grim prognosis. I've received texts with pictures of shiny headstones instead of smiling selfies. I've comforted friends as they've lost their homes and their jobs, their marriages and their parents.

Perhaps you're dealing with a personal tragedy you never saw coming. Perhaps someone you love is. Perhaps you're struggling to understand the view from your window as our culture morphs into something you don't even recognize anymore. Or maybe life's inevitable ordeals and daily frustrations are slowly eating away at your soul one little bite at a time.

Following Jesus doesn't exempt us from earth-shattering, heart-breaking events in our own homes. We still have cancer and car accidents. Our kids are still suicidal; our marriages are still struggling. Our parents still have Alzheimer's. Our loved ones are still making bad decisions with big consequences.

These are the moments when our faith in God collides with real life and crises pile up like cars on an icy interstate. When life as we know it is upended and disrupted, we crawl through the ambiguity like a car with a burned-out headlight. We drift between the lanes of dark hopelessness and dim hopefulness:

> It's hopeless; she'll never get better.
> *Hopefully, we have one more Christmas.*

> It's hopeless; this marriage is over.
> *Hopefully, the rumors aren't true.*

> It's hopeless; my prodigal is too far gone.
> *Hopefully, my son will be safe.*

> It's hopeless; I'll never be out of debt.
> *Hopefully, I'll find a job soon.*

In seasons of uncertainty and anguish, a catchy Bible verse on a T-shirt or cute wall art from Hobby Lobby just doesn't cut it. How does God's hope-filled plan for your future work when your life is falling apart (Jeremiah 29:11)? Did he take a wrong turn as his hand guided you to a place you never wanted to go (Psalm 139:10)? Did he get the memo about that urgent thing you needed, like, yesterday (Matthew 6:25)?

These tests of my faith feel like drinking from a teacup while driving through a pileup, trying not to spill a single drop. My dreams slosh over the sides and stain my carefully laid plans until my cup is dry.

Can I borrow a cup of hope?

Know Peter, Know Jesus

The New Testament book of 1 Peter is where we'll learn how to find faith for hard times and refill our sloshed-over, drained-dry cups with abundant hope. This letter from the apostle Peter to the first Christians comprises only 105 verses, five short chapters, and maybe three or four thin pages in your Bible. But even though it's short, as you get to know Peter, his words will become as comforting as a personal note from a dear friend. In his letter, Peter will help us set aside our hopeless fears and hopeful fantasies and instead set our hope fully on God's faithfulness. We want to know Peter so we can know Jesus.

Peter watched as his hopes and dreams were hauled away in handcuffs, then crucified and buried. When Peter didn't handle himself well, he created a whole new set of problems. Key events of Peter's life story, embarrassingly well-documented in Scripture for all to see, are a series of contradictions. Sure, he walked on water . . . and sank like a cinder block. Peter boldly proclaimed he was Jesus's most loyal follower . . . and that same night denied he even knew him. Peter's world was divided between hopefulness and hopelessness, trust and fear, confidence and uncertainty, comfortable "old normal" and terrifying "new normal." Peter summited the highest spiritual peaks then plunged into deep valleys of failure—sometimes on the same day. If you can relate to someone who does everything wrong before they finally get it right, you'll come to love him like I do. "He is just like you and me, only more so," wrote musician and author Michael Card.[1]

Peter was also fully forgiven by Jesus and restored to the friends who'd been eyewitnesses to his downfall. He became a pillar of the early church and is revered as an apostle today. Once a denier of Christ, Peter never again stopped talking about his Savior! Peter lived for the glory of God, and that's also how he died. Peter's passing isn't included in Scripture, but we'll learn how historians say he and his wife raised a toast with their cups of hope as they faced death together.

How It Works

Working sequentially through Peter's letter, we will find solid hope to sustain you through life's storms. The first-century advice Peter gave to the early church can be applied and be useful to your present-day relationships. Each chapter of this book will help you navigate the hurts and hardships that have detoured the plans you meticulously mapped out. You'll learn to react to chaos and confusion with calm, clearheaded, Christlike responses. You'll even learn five Peter-inspired coping strategies to use when your world is turned upside down in a chapter called "How to Survive the End of the World." That's where you'll discover a prayer that never fails and see how it helps us win the ultimate victory in every ordeal. You'll also be encouraged by five modern-day women who are facing great sorrow with incredible grace. Finally, using Peter as your role model, you'll shed the shame of past mistakes and see God's glory in your story.

You can read this book straight through without taking a breath if you'd like. I hope you'll mark it up and make notes in the margins. (I always read a book with a pencil in my hand.) There are questions at the end of each lesson for reflection, discussion, and further study called "A Second Cup," in case you want just a little bit more. I'd suggest purchasing a journal where you can record any insights and respond to that deeper section. By the time you reach the end, you will be able to understand unsettling current events through the lens of faith and apply practical biblical wisdom to your daily life.

You can also use this book as a Bible study to do on your own or with a group of friends. Each chapter is divided into five lessons; if you read one lesson every weekday, you'll complete one chapter a week for a six-week Bible study. Each member of the group will want a journal to keep track of their answers to "A Second Cup." The Second Cup questions for lesson 1 in each chapter start off light and conversational—there are no wrong answers!—to break the ice if you're reading this book with a group. Then the Second Cup delves deeper into Scripture and real-life application. While the lessons stick to the book of 1 Peter and Peter's life recorded in the Gospels and Acts, the Second Cup will cover Scripture from all over the Bible. Since a small group won't usually have time to talk about every Second Cup question, look for the questions with a black cup to guide rich conversation in a gathering of friends.

I want to make it as easy as possible for you to get into God's Word, so all the Scripture references in this book are available at www .amylively.com/cup-of-hope (along with lots of online bonus content!). At the beginning of each of the six chapters, you'll find scannable codes that will quickly take you to the Bible reading. Simply open the camera app on your smartphone and point it at the code, then tap the banner that appears on the screen (or if you're reading an ebook, just tap the code to open the link). Give it a try right now:

You can also use *Can I Borrow a Cup of Hope?* as a devotional. A short prayer, intended to ease your sorrow as you lean into the suffering of Christ, concludes each lesson. Together we're going to discover how to transform uncertain seasons of fear and confusion into a new normal full of hope and purpose!

I've been studying 1 Peter for over a decade (I'm a slow learner!). Each verse has spoken to me in different ways at various times, sometimes waking me in the middle of the night with a fresh application for a new problem. Most of the time, Peter tells me exactly what I *don't* want to hear. I don't want to be silent when I'm offended; I want to give a snarky reply. I don't want to bless people who hurt me; I want to hurt them right back. And I definitely don't want to endure suffering; I want it to end, right now.

I sense it's the same for you.

Here's hope, friend.

The end of the world as you know it is only the beginning of Jesus.

A SECOND CUP

 Can you find your way without GPS, or are you directionally challenged like me? Share about a time when you were lost in a strange place or when your travel arrangements didn't go as planned.

 Read Jeremiah 29:11, Psalm 139:7–12, and Matthew 6:25–34.

If Jeremiah 29:11 is true, your future is _____.

If Psalm 139:10 is correct, God is _____.

If Matthew 6:32 is right, God knows _____.

 Can you think of a time when your faith had a head-on collision with a real-life crisis and these verses felt insufficient—or even untrue?

 Read the book of 1 Peter. It's only five chapters, 105 verses, just a few pages in your Bible.

Dear heavenly Father, please reveal your Son to me during my suffering and open your Word to me in new ways. I need your grace more than ever, and I am desperate for your hope. In Jesus's name, amen.

CHAPTER 1

HEAVEN AND THE HERE AND NOW

1 Peter 1

"What time is it, Mama?" Emma asked from the back seat. I told her it was five o'clock. "No, it's not," she scolded me. "It's 4:59. Why do you lie to me? It makes me feel like I can't trust you."

This saying has remained a family joke since our then-kindergartner learned how to tell time, but it took me a while to realize how often I ask God the same question. "What time is this problem going to end, Lord? Were you lying when you said you had plans for a good future filled with hope? When you don't give me the exact answer I'm expecting, it makes me feel like I can't trust you!"

When unwelcome trials and troubles destroy our carefully constructed timelines, our hope floats right out the window. Happiness, peace, and security pack their bags and take the next bus out of town. In uncertain seasons of personal crisis, national chaos, or global catastrophe, we distrust God's timing and doubt his good intentions.

Peter got what that is like. He had left everything to follow a new rabbi—his home with his wife, his career as a commercial fisherman, his community in Capernaum on the shore of the Sea of Galilee—and his work with Jesus was drawing attention. Jesus liked Peter so much that he gave him a special nickname and even hinted at a future promotion, something about being the foundation of a new organization (Matthew 16:18). Then Peter went from a hopeful future to a hopeless failure overnight. His hope didn't just fade away: it was arrested, crucified, and buried. To make matters worse, Peter publicly failed every test of his faith—and each mistake was witnessed by his entire community and written down, ensuring no one would ever forget his failure.

One day you're living your best life and the next you're facing your worst fears. But do you know one thing I love about Jesus? He allows us—encourages us even—to ask hard questions when we're hurting. "Are you really who you say you are? Can you be trusted? Are you still here? When are you going to make things right?"

His answer is always, "Yes! I'm still watching over you, and I'm here in the waiting with you. I'm by your side and on your side for all time, forevermore." God takes a longer view of time than a kindergartener's view of an hour when she is first learning how to read the clock. The minute between 4:59 and 5:00 is no different to God than the millennium between 459 BC and AD 500.

God's never-changing character and never-ending calendar are the theme we're going to uncover in the first chapter of 1 Peter. Whenever we read a verse or phrase about God's eternal timeline, draw a simple illustration of a clock beside it, like this:

Come with me to meet Simon Peter and the recipients of his letter and to understand why they were just as shocked as we are by his advice to rejoice in suffering. Together we'll unpack the living hope Peter wants us to have and see what a difference it makes when we insert just enough space between *hopefully* and *hope fully* to allow God's power to enter in. Then Peter's mysterious wife will make her first appearance! Finally, you'll be inspired and encouraged when you meet my good, godly girlfriend Michelle, as you read the story of how she has kept her eyes on Jesus during suffering and loss.

 Scan this code or visit www.amylively.com/cup-of-hope /#chapter1 to access online resources and read the Scripture passages online.

Lesson 1

— ❊ —

Say Hello to Simon Peter

Read 1 Peter 1:1–5

I HAD WALKED AWAY FROM God for twenty years (more on that later). But now I was back, fully in love with Jesus and eagerly walking in his ways. A friend invited me to a Wednesday night Bible study at her church where she introduced me to her pastor and his wife (more on them later, too). We didn't get far that evening; in fact, the pastor only covered the first three words of the book they were starting:

Peter, an apostle . . . (1 Peter 1:1)

So that's how I met Peter, and as the weeks of the Bible study continued, I realized more and more how his story sounded a lot like mine—a follower of Jesus who had a major fall from grace. I was curious to see how that turned out for him (and maybe for me).

Peter answered to several names. His given name was Simon, which means "hearing with acceptance, or to hear and understand."[1] Simon was a common Hebrew name, and there are at least nine different men named Simon in the New Testament. Jesus, speaking a language called

Aramaic, gave our Simon the title of Cephas (kay-*fas*), which means rock.[2] The New Testament was written in the Greek language, which translates Cephas ("rock") as *Petros* ("rock"). In English, we say Peter.

Whatever you call him, the meanings of Peter's names are significant in his testimony. For example, Simon—"to hear and understand"—is similar to the definition of *disciple*, meaning a student who hears Jesus's teaching, listens and understands, then follows and obeys. Peter was the first to proclaim that he understood that Jesus was the Christ, the son of the living God; he was also called the rock upon which Christ would build the church. Peter's names tell a story about his character.

Before Peter became an apostle ("special messenger") of Jesus Christ, he was a disciple—the first one Jesus called. Peter is always named first when Jesus's twelve core disciples are listed. But Jesus also had many faithful female disciples who are named in the New Testament, and we still name our daughters after them today: Anna, Joanna, Lois, Lydia, Martha, Phoebe, Priscilla, Suzanna, Tabitha, and of course Mary, Mary, Mary, Mary, Mary, and Mary—there are a lot of Marys!

One woman who is not named in Scripture is Peter's wife. We know Peter had a wife because he had a mother-in-law who was healed by Jesus. We also know from Paul's writing that the apostles' wives traveled with them, and he specifically referenced Peter's wife (1 Corinthians 9:5). Although Peter's wife's name is never given, her marriage with Peter was likely the model for his writing about women, husbands, and wives, which we'll study together. And if being married for over thirty years myself has taught me anything, I'll bet she proofread this letter to the early church before Peter mailed it.

Peter's wife would have wondered why he was late getting home from work the day he met Jesus, because she was probably waiting for his fresh catch from the sea to prepare their dinner. Jesus stayed at her home and knew her name, and she would have hugged him tight after he touched and healed her mother. It's quite likely she was at the Last

Supper with the other disciples' families. She would have held Peter as he wept after betraying Jesus, she was probably hiding with him in the upper room after the crucifixion, and she surely would have rejoiced with her husband when he was reaffirmed by Jesus after his resurrection. She would have been worried for Peter when he was in prison, and she traveled with him while he ministered to the church and wrote his letters. We'll read all these stories about Peter in upcoming lessons.

Elect Exiles

After identifying himself as "Peter, an apostle," Peter addressed this letter:

> To those who are elect exiles of the Dispersion in Pontus, Galatia, Cappadocia, Asia, and Bithynia . . . (1 Peter 1:1)

Located in modern-day Turkey, these regions are listed from east to west. While there aren't any references in the Bible to Peter having traveled to these regions, it's possible that he was writing to people he met as he passed through on his way from Jerusalem to Rome. The Emperor Claudius (AD 41–54) colonized all five of these regions to create routes for commerce, develop a strong military presence, and expand Roman culture (read: money, power, and control). It was common Roman practice to fill up new territories with merchants, military veterans, and slaves (along with a few troublemakers, foreigners, and others who were perceived as disruptive).[3] This territory was full of Christians who had been forced to relocate their families across the Roman Empire and now found themselves far from home in hostile environments.

Archaeologists recently unearthed an entire city hidden beneath the earth in the modern-day Turkish city of Midyat, located near the region known as Cappadocia in Peter's time. This underground network of caves included interconnected chambers used as anything from homes to wells for water, to silos for storing grain. Although only partially excavated, archaeologists believe the colossal complex could have housed up to seventy thousand people! Known as Matiate, which means "City of Caves," the excavated area was also found to contain "a Christian church and a large hall with a Star of David symbol on the wall."[4] Archaeologists believe Matiate may have been used by Christians seeking refuge from the persecution of Rome in the second or third century. Can you imagine if committing your life to Christ meant moving your family to an underground cave city just to survive persecution?

Yet Peter calls them *elect*. They were carefully chosen and specially selected to be cast out of their comfort zone, evicted from their spiritual homeland in Jerusalem, and scattered into strange, dark places. "Elect exiles" is an oxymoron, two contradictory terms that don't go together—like giant shrimp, deafening silence, civil war, or social distancing. "Elect exiles" is a paradox that only makes sense in Christ's upside-down kingdom where the first are last, we die to live, and we're carefully chosen and specially selected for suffering. (If that's confusing or hurtful, please hang on until we get to 1 Peter 2.)

We're not just talking about first-century Christians anymore, are we? We are all exiles, tired travelers who are watching the clock and wondering, "Are we there yet? How much longer?" With a longing for heaven imprinted in our DNA (Ecclesiastes 3:11), our hearts can never be fully satisfied with the here and now. God uses earthly scenes of beauty and every second of suffering to turn our hearts toward our one true home. Until then, he gives us grace and peace as the minutes slowly tick by.

Grace and Peace

Both Peter's contemporaries and scholars today don't quite understand how a fisherman from a poor Jewish village became such a sharp theologian, but this short letter has been called "one of the noblest books in the New Testament"[5] and is one of the most often preached books in the Bible.[6] In fact, by the second verse, Peter has packed in so much important doctrine that you could spend a lifetime studying it. Our fisherman's pen captures the entire Trinity in a single Scripture:

> According to the foreknowledge of *God the Father*,
> in the sanctification of the *Spirit*,
> for obedience to *Jesus Christ*
> and for sprinkling with his blood:
> May grace and peace be multiplied to you. (1 Peter 1:2)

Before he invented time by separating the day from the night, your Father knew you. He planned this day for you—right here, right now—before the first sunrise in Eden. He knew you, and he saw you, and oh sweet friend, how he loved you—even then. And especially now.

The Holy Spirit is the whisper of Jesus to your soul, reminding you of everything Christ said and did and taught by his example. When you are a believer in Jesus, the Spirit lives within you, giving you strength and energy, counsel and encouragement and helping you to grow in your faith, understand your purpose, and carry out God's will for your life.

When you're a believer, you're free and fully able to obey all Jesus Christ's commands . . . and there must be a lot of them, right, if your obedience came at such a high price? Nope: just two—love God and love your neighbor. And you're not even expected to muster up this affection on your own! The love of the Father flows through Christ's outstretched arms on the cross, where he shed his blood for you. Through the chalice of his Spirit, Christ's love is poured into your heart so it can flow back to him and to others.

As God's children, we can experience what Peter wishes for us to have overflowing abundantly in every part of our lives—grace, the good things we don't deserve, and peace, that inexplicable feeling of confidence and calmn even when everything is falling apart around us.

Wow, that's a lot! Did you get all that? Do you understand how the whole Holy Trinity operates? Don't worry. You don't need a seminary degree to experience God working in your ordinary life. The Father, Spirit, and Son delight to help you love God with all your heart, soul, and strength and love your neighbor as yourself.

Born Again to a Living Hope

This sweet knowledge of the Trinity makes Peter (and us) burst into spontaneous praise!

> Blessed be the God and Father of our Lord Jesus Christ! According to his great mercy, he has caused us to be born again to a living hope through the resurrection of Jesus Christ from the dead. (1 Peter 1:3)

If you've ever wondered where that churchy phrase "born again" comes from, here it is. The Amplified translation of this verse nicely defines what it means to be born again:

> [To be reborn from above—spiritually transformed, renewed, and set apart for His purpose] to an ever-living hope and confident assurance. (1 Peter 1:3 AMP)

God's mercy gives us a second chance at life, made possible by the death and resurrection of his Son. When we're born again, we receive a hope-filled infusion of Christ's blood that he shed on the cross. If you believe that Jesus Christ is the Son of God who was crucified for the forgiveness of your sins, then rose from the dead so you could have a living hope, then you, friend, are born again. Mark it down in your planner, repeat it out loud, and never forget it: "I am at peace with God. I am born again."

To be a born-again believer in Christ comes with all kinds of perks. Peter describes it so:

To an inheritance that is imperishable, undefiled, and unfading, kept in heaven for you, who by God's power are being guarded through faith for a salvation ready to be revealed in the last time. (1 Peter 1:4–5)

Heaven is for real, Peter writes, and that future day and place is when God will finally and fully reveal the joy of our salvation and our inheritance as his children. Later, much later than now, we'll have it all—Jesus, face-to-face. Our Father, wiping away our tears. His church, without the brokenness. Today we just get a little sneak peek. Remember that clock we drew at the beginning of this chapter? Draw a clock beside this verse in your Bible to remember that God's power protects us until the coming day when his strong arms embrace us.

A SECOND CUP

 What is the meaning of your name? What is your nickname, or what is your name in another language? How has the meaning of your name proven significant in your life?

 Have you ever moved to a new community? How did you make friends? What did you do if you felt alone, isolated, or even exiled?

 Think of a time when you experienced grace and peace— *grace*, something good you don't deserve; and *peace*, confidence and calmness even when everything is falling

apart. How does this help you trust God's hand in your present circumstances?

If you're watching the clock and wondering when God is going to show up, you are not alone. Many times in the book of Psalms the writer cries out, "How long, O Lord?" before remembering God's faithfulness. For each of these psalms, record in your journal how the psalmist feels about their situation and the fact about God that gives them comfort.

Psalm	Feeling	Fact
13	Verses 1–2	Verses 5–6
35	Verse 17	Verse 27
74	Verses 9–11	Verses 12–17
94	Verses 3–7	Verses 9–11
119	Verses 82–84	Verses 86–88

How do you feel as you wait for God to come through for you? What facts about God's unchanging character bring comfort to you?

Dear heavenly Father, thank you for grace and peace as I wait for you. Even when I feel all alone, I know you are near. Help me to stay strong until I receive all you have promised me. In Jesus's name, amen.

Lesson 2

 ✦

Rejoice! Wait. What?

Read 1 Peter 1:6–12, 20–21

THERE'S AN INCONVENIENT TRUTH RIGHT at the beginning of 1 Peter that I would rather avoid. Right after his glorious description of our new life and living hope, Peter drops this truth bomb:

> In this you rejoice, though now for a little while, if necessary, you have been grieved by various trials. (1 Peter 1:6)

I wish following Jesus would make everything better and all our problems go away, but here's one Bible promise you can count on: you will have hard times and grief, trials and tests, sorrows and sufferings.

I'm sorry to be the bearer of bad news, but you already knew this, didn't you? You've felt it, you've lived it, you know it deep in your soul. Let's be honest: Sometimes it's easier to hope in heaven rather than the here and now, easier to imagine walking down streets of gold than walking through another hard day. And another. And another. Sometimes the suffering seems endless, not to mention pointless. How can it be that those end-of-the-world-as-we-know-it, TEOTWAWKI moments—when life disintegrates before our eyes—are fleeting, light, and momentary, and even *necessary?*

When we place our present suffering on God's eternal timeline, we may start to feel like our pain is insignificant in the grand scheme of things. We may start to wonder, Is my unimaginable pain a trivial thing to God? Is it just a blip—a candle in the galaxy of stars, a fleck of dust in the earth's atmosphere, a single grain of sand on an endless beach? Does God see? Does he care? And when in the world will he intervene? God's timepiece seems broken during round-the-clock suffering.

Oh, sweetheart, God knows! Like physical exercise that hurts today and prepares us to compete tomorrow, these various, grievous trials do serve an important purpose. Draw a clock beside verse 6 on the previous page, by the words "now for a little while" to remind yourself that suffering now will end later.

We suffer so that

the *tested* genuineness of your faith—more precious than gold that perishes though it is tested by fire—may be found to *result* in praise and glory and honor at the revelation of Jesus Christ. (1 Peter 1:7)

We all know what it's like to wait for a test result. Anyone who has peed on a pregnancy stick, had a needle stuck into a mysterious mass, or had a cotton swab shoved way too far up their nostril knows the anticipation of waiting. As far as the test of suffering goes, the results are a faith that is real, worship that is genuine, and praise that reaches the heavens. From his throne, God hears our precious prayers and reminds us that he can tell time. He just doesn't tell us *exactly* what time he's going to reveal the results and outcomes of our trials and the purpose of our pain. Our trials today prove God's faithfulness as he comes through time and time again. They purify our hearts and purge our doubts as we become firsthand witnesses to God's Word working in each circumstance. So although our trials feel like a race we didn't know we were running (we didn't even get the T-shirt!), they train us. The praise and glory and honor we bring to Jesus during our pain put our suffering in perspective and bring it into focus, like being fitted for glasses that finally have the right prescription.

Through the lens of eternity, the light from a single candle can be seen from the next planet over. We see how a cloud forms around that fleck of dust in the sky and rains down showers of blessing. And our eyes watch in wonder as that tiny grain of sand on an endless beach slips into an oyster and becomes a glistening pearl. Your Father will redeem, reclaim, and repurpose your sadness. He will be with you while it lasts for "a little while," even if it feels like forever. That's a promise you can set your clock by.

When You Can't See Jesus

I recently saw a movie scene depicting happy New Year partiers wearing eyeglasses shaped like the number 2020 and dancing and singing in Times Square. It honestly felt like watching innocent, unsuspecting people board the *Titanic*. I wanted to shout a warning: "Wait! Stop! Enjoy 2019 while you can! You have no idea what's coming!" The year 2020 gave us perfect 20/20 hindsight, as we looked back longingly and wished for:

Hugs we should have given; words we should have spoken.
Phone calls we should have placed; visits we should have made.
Apologies we should have accepted; forgiveness we should have extended.
Money we should have saved; bills we should have paid.
Unfairness we should have uncovered; injustice we should have confronted.

When we aren't regretfully looking back, we stare into the future with a strange concoction of hopeful anticipation, fear, and dread. But if you're stuck wistfully looking back or anxiously peering ahead, you might miss the grace offered in the painful, present moment.

> Though you have not seen him, you love him. Though you do not now see him, you believe in him and rejoice with joy that is inexpressible and filled with glory, obtaining the outcome of your faith, the salvation of your souls. (1 Peter 1:8–9)

There may come a time in your life when Jesus will fail to meet the expectations you have of him. Perhaps the hopes and dreams you've conjured up in your heart will not materialize as they do in the last ninety seconds of a Hallmark Christmas movie as you wish they would. Christ may have seemed distant when you needed him close and begged for his comforting presence. But Peter reminds us that until we have really and truly set our eyes on Jesus, we're relying on our own imperfect vision and distorted perception, watching the clock with our limited understanding of timelines and deadlines. Let's listen to Peter explain how to love and trust Jesus even when our hearts are filled with doubt and we don't quite understand what he's up to.

Who, What, Where, Why, and When?

We aren't the first to wonder who, what, where, why, and when God is going to come through. In 1 Peter 1:10–12 we read that the Old Testament prophets "searched and inquired carefully" about God's mysterious mix of suffering, redemption, grace, salvation, and glory.

Those poor prophets. God asked them to do some crazy things! Isaiah was told to walk around naked for three years; Hosea was ordered to take back his adulterous wife; and Ezekiel had to lay on his left side for 390 days, then on his right side for 40 days while eating a morsel of bread cooked over a pile of poo (Isaiah 20; Hosea 3; Ezekiel 4). You can't make this stuff up! First Peter 1:12 says that even the angels were wondering what was going on. You can bet the prophets asked the age-old question: "Why?" They wanted to know when they'd get to the glory part, and how it would ever make sense. And do you know how the Lord answered them? He pointed them to Jesus.

Jump ahead a few verses and you'll see the purpose of Jesus's suffering:

> [Christ] was foreknown before the foundation of the world but was made manifest in the last times *for the sake of you* who through him are believers in God, who raised him from the dead and gave him glory, *so that* your faith and hope are in God. (1 Peter 1:20–21)

In ages past, long before Planet Earth was ever set in the sky, the Father planned to reveal his Son for *your* sake. For you. For us. You are Jesus's *why*, his purpose, that helped him hang on when they hung him on a cross. Because of him, we believe in God. Your *faith* is not confidence that a mystical being will grant your wishes, and your *hope* is not optimism that everything will turn out okay. Our faith and hope are *in God*—not in good times, perfect outcomes, or happily-ever-after endings. And God's clock is set on Eternity Savings Time.

A SECOND CUP

 Tell about a time when your rejoicing was interrupted by an unexpected trial, as described in 1 Peter 1:6. When have you seen Jesus working in your sadness? How do you identify with the prophets who didn't understand what was happening to them?

Read Psalm 90. This "Prayer of Moses" is thought to be one of the oldest psalms in the Bible. What is Moses's unique perspective about time in this psalm?

 Compare Psalm 90:4 and 2 Peter 3:8 by writing them side by side in your journal. How does this compare to your view of time? What does 2 Peter 3:9 tell us about God's purpose if it seems like he's taking a long time to fulfill some of his promises?

 Write out Psalm 90:12 on a notecard or a sticky note and post it by a clock where you'll see it several times a day. What is one thing you would do differently today if you knew you only had a few days left? What is one step you can take toward that goal *today*?

Dear heavenly Father, I confess that it can be hard to see Jesus when I'm really hurting. When my faith is being tried, I want to pass the test! As I walk through life's fires, please purify me and help me to praise you.
In Jesus's name, amen.

—— ✷ ——

Hope Fully

Read 1 Peter 1:13

WHENEVER THE WORD *THEREFORE* APPEARS at the beginning of a Bible verse, Sunday school students around the globe chime in unison, "What's it there *for*?" We see it at the beginning of verse 13, the verse that stopped me in my tracks until I wrote an entire book about it:

> Therefore, preparing your minds for action, and being sober-minded, set your hope fully on the grace that will be brought to you at the revelation of Jesus Christ. (1 Peter 1:13)

"Therefore" is there for what came before it, so to really understand 1 Peter 1:13 we must look back at verses 1–12.

- *Therefore*, even though we feel off-kilter and out of place in this crazy world (verse 1), the Father, Spirit, and Son are deeply involved in our daily lives (verse 2).
- *Therefore*, we are born again to a living hope, a logical hope, a hope that is accessible, real, and powerful (verse 3) right here, right now.

- *Therefore*, our hope will never wither or waste away (verse 4), and God is protecting us now for heaven later (verse 5).
- *Therefore*, our hope is fixed and firm, eternal—our trials and troubles are shifting, temporary, light, and momentary (verse 6).
- *Therefore*, our tested, genuine, refined, and purified faith brings praise and glory and honor as Jesus Christ is revealed through the shimmer of our tears (verse 7).
- *Therefore*, we breathe a sigh of relief as we release our hopeful wishes and dreams into the hands that hold the stars in the sky and cradle our hope fully, safely, and securely (verse 8).
- *Therefore*, even though we don't see Jesus beside us in the flesh, we love him and believe in him with great joy (verses 8–9).
- *Therefore*, we wait patiently for God to reveal his good timing as we trust his good intentions (verses 10–12).

That's what the *therefore* is there for. Hallelujah!

Therefore, we prepare our minds for action. The Greek word Peter used for "preparing" is obscure. *Anazōnnymi* (an-ad-*zone*-noo-mee) means to "gird up" or put on a girdle (or your Spanx). Men in Peter's culture (and still around the world today) wore long, loose, layered tunics that allowed air to circulate and provided insulation from the heat. This worked great on a hot desert day but wasn't so great for going into battle. When they needed to ride a camel or run after an enemy, they tucked the tunic into a belt worn around their waist. I don't know why they didn't just wear pants, which were invented a thousand years before Christ. Today we might say "put on your big girl pants," but my cowgirl friend Gwen would have said, "Saddle up!" In other words, get ready and do something!

Peter is the only New Testament writer to use this "Saddle up!" word. When the Greeks translated the Old Testament from Hebrew in a version of the Bible called the Septuagint, this word was used two other times: once for men armed for war (Judges 18:16) and the other for women armed with strength. You know this famous lady from Proverbs 31:

> She *equips herself* with strength [spiritual, mental, and physical fitness for her God-given task] and makes her arms strong. (Proverbs 31:17 AMP)

Equipping yourself with strength and girding your mind for action require self-control and self-discipline, regular practice and repetition. No one else can go to the gym and lift weights for you. You won't get results if you pay for the gym membership or buy the fitness app but never do the hard, sweaty work of picking heavy things up and putting them back down or elevating your heart rate above an easy sedentary pace. God offers endless strength through his Spirit, but you won't achieve results if you sit in the pew or sign up for the Bible study and never do the work. Preparing for action, even in the mind, takes hard work, sweat, and often tears.

Peter used a pair of words, combining "Saddle up!" with "Get serious!" To be sober-minded (Greek *nēphō*, pronounced *nay*-fo) means not to be drunk with wine; it also means serious, sensible, and solemn. This word is used only six times in the New Testament—three in 1 Peter—and he always paired it with another word:

1. Preparing your minds for action, and being sober-minded. (1:13)
2. Be self-controlled and sober-minded for the sake of your prayers. (4:7)
3. Be sober-minded; be watchful. Your adversary the devil prowls around like a roaring lion, seeking someone to devour. (5:8)

What does it look like to be sober-minded as well as mentally prepared, self-controlled, and watchful? Picture yourself at a bar—not a classy hotel bar but a seedy back-alley bar. It's dark and smoky, dangerous. You're in a booth with your back to the wall so no one can sneak up behind you. You're sipping water—no margaritas for you tonight. With your chin high, your eyes scan the room for signs of trouble. You've got one hand on your bag in case you need to bolt for the door—but you can't leave, because this bar is real life. You live here. This bar is the big, bad world, and if you're not sober-minded and wearing your big girl pants, you're going to be sucked in and taken down. Letting your thoughts run wild is like having the bartender refill your glass with whiskey until you pass out.

Or you can take control. You have the ability and the responsibility to control your thoughts, monitor your desires, and direct your emotions. You can choose the thoughts inside your own head as much as you pick out an outfit to wear each day. You are in charge of your own mind.

Oh, What a Difference a Space Makes

If you've ever teetered between hopelessness and hopefulness like Peter—and like me—you'll understand this guy. Peter messed up royally. Then he was redeemed and restored. He traveled a long, hard road to earn his position of respect in the early church, whose members had seen his failures and mistakes firsthand. They also watched as an uneducated, untrained, impulsive, and even reckless fisherman was filled with the Holy Spirit and was transformed into a bold preacher who could be trusted to write these words:

> Therefore, preparing your minds for action, and being sober-minded, set your *hope fully* on the grace that will be brought to you at the revelation of Jesus Christ. (1 Peter 1:13)

Oh, what a difference a space makes! Instead of flickering between hopeless fears and hopeful fantasies, Peter sets our hope fully on God's faithfulness. *Hopefully* is just an expression of my desired outcome for my current circumstances based upon my feelings. Grammatically, *hopefully* tells you how I feel about the rest of the sentence. It's structurally dispensable: you can toss it out and lose nothing except the speaker's emotion about the real subject. *Hopefully* is an adverb that describes how I feel about what I'm about to say.

To *hope fully* means so much more.

Hope (Greek *elpizō*, pronounced el-*pid*-zo) encompasses all your expectations, confidence, assurance, and anticipation. Peter describes it as a "living hope" (verse 3)—the King James Version says it's a "lively hope," that's my favorite!—that is active, alive, full of breath, fresh, strong, efficient, powerful, and thriving. Hope isn't a wish; it's a grounded reality based on the promises of God. Hope isn't a longing; it's a knowing.

To hope *fully* means your confidence, trust, and reliance is perfectly, completely, entirely, and steadfastly established and rooted in Jesus Christ. Hope isn't an escape from reality; it's a real person.

To *set* your hope fully on Christ requires forward-thinking, preplanned, self-disciplined, self-controlled, clearheaded decision-making. We direct our minds and our wills to control our emotions, not the other way around. We don't sit idly by while our world unravels; we implement a spiritual strategy (and oh, yes, Peter is going to show you how!). Hope isn't a baseless claim; it's a battle plan.

This hope is set fully on the *grace* God brings. Grace is a gift from God's hand to your heart, carefully chosen to meet your exact need and given at the exact moment you need it. Grace is a present filled with God's kindness, goodness, and loveliness wrapped with a big bow of everlasting life. Hope isn't a flimsy wish; it's a never-ending gift.

We set our hope fully on the grace given as Christ is *revealed*. God doesn't always reveal the miracle we are longing for. Instead, he reveals the miraculous presence of Jesus Christ amid our sorrow and pain. Hope isn't an outcome; it's a joy no matter what comes.

When we look at difficult trials through this lens, we experience a paradigm shift in our approach to suffering. After we cry, "Why are you doing this to me?" we can ask, "How can you use me?" Instead of running away, we head into the fire. Instead of planning our escape, we become intercessors for others. Instead of self-pity, we notice the by-standers watching how we handle the grief, the agony, the outrage. We surrender our suffering and allow our lives to become a living sacrifice, poured out and emptied yet refilled with joy as God reveals himself day after excruciating day. We trust him to work through the struggles that draw us to the cross, the gut-punch of pain that pushes us to our knees in prayer, and the long, hard seasons of suffering that sweeten our worship.

That's how Peter lived. That's how Peter died, too, and you'll be amazed when you read the story of his final hours in the next lesson. As many times as Peter utterly failed to follow his own advice, he ultimately glorified God to the very end. The lessons Peter learned from his many mistakes qualify him to be our teacher. He will show us how to pry apart our *hopeless* and *hopeful* emotions and how to invite God's power to enter in the tiny space between these impassioned words.

If you were born on Planet Earth, Peter and I can both guarantee you'll wake up to a new problem or two every day. When you do, there is hope.

Hope is not based on happy circumstances or rosy outcomes. Hope is more than getting what we want, when we want it, with a cherry on top. Hope is not a wish for a happy ending someday. Hope is a decision to trust God today.

When "hopefully" fails, hope fully in Jesus.

A SECOND CUP

 Choose a method that suits your learning style to help you memorize 1 Peter 1:13:

- Print each phrase on a separate card that you can flip through as you repeat them.
- Place the cards around the room so you can move around as you study them.
- Write the verse several times and then read it back to yourself until you can repeat it.
- Speak the verse aloud until it sticks. Make a song out of it!
- Have someone quiz you to see how well you've memorized the verse.
- Download a free wallpaper for your phone screen with the verse at www.amylively.com/hope-wallpaper, or scan this code:

 Do you agree or disagree with the statement, "You have the ability and the responsibility to control your thoughts, monitor your desires, and direct your emotions"? How does the concept of choosing our own thoughts change how we might deal with a difficult situation?

 Whenever you catch yourself using the word *hopefully* in a sentence, see if you could truthfully substitute *hope fully* no matter how it turns out.

 Read Hebrews 11:1. What is the connection between hope and faith? What words are used to describe faith and hope?

Although faith and hope are "not seen," how do you see them working together in your life?

Dear heavenly Father, my hope is in you! When my mind is clouded, help me to think clearly. My only plan during uncertain times is to trust in you, because my hope fully rests on your grace! In Jesus's name, amen.

Lesson 4

O Thou, Remember the Lord

Read 1 Peter 1:13–19

W‌HEN I WAS GROWING UP, one of my dad's favorite ways to encourage me to do something I didn't want to do, like clean my room, eat my vegetables, or be nice to my brother, was to tell me, "It'll put hair on your chest!" I did not then, nor do I now, want hair on my chest. These character-building exercises may have been good for me, but I preferred my unmade bed, candy for dinner, and not sharing my toys.

It's against my human nature to ask God for what I need instead of what I want. My prayers are pretty much like, "Please make all these things better, make us happy and healthy, shower us with good things, keep the blessings flowing, and keep us safe, in Jesus's name, amen. PS: If you could do that *right now*, that would be good." Or maybe that's just me?

But Peter? He's asking for grace. In 1 Peter 1:13, Peter tells us to purposefully and intentionally set our hope fully on God's grace. God's grace doesn't mean we get everything we want to be happy; it means we get exactly what we need to be holy. In Greek, the word Peter used for grace is *charis* and it's the gift God gives us so that we can develop the character of Christ:

Charis (khar-ece): good will, lovingkindness, favor, the merciful kindness by which God, exerting his holy influence upon souls, turns them to Christ, keeps, strengthens, increases them in Christian faith, knowledge, affection, and kindles them to the exercise of the Christian virtues.[7]

God's grace can be trusted, and his gifts are always good—even if they're not exactly what we had in mind:

> *Instead of ending the crisis, he gives endurance.*
> *Instead of material things, he gives contentment.*
> *Instead of health, he gives peace.*
> *Instead of happiness, he gives holiness.*
> *Instead of answers, he gives patience.*
> *Instead of prosperity, he gives purity.*
> *Instead of immediacy, he gives intimacy.*

When we cry out for the easy way out, God's got bigger, better, holier things in mind.

The Perfect Disposition

Peter's death wasn't recorded in the Bible, but historical writings from the first century tell us he was crucified. These reports tell us that Peter didn't think he was worthy of being killed in the same manner as Christ, so he asked to be crucified upside down. An early church historian named Eusebius referenced the traditional view that Peter and his wife were both martyred for their faith in Christ on the same day:

> When the blessed Peter saw his own wife led out to die, he rejoiced because of her summons and her return home, and called to her very encouragingly and comfortingly, addressing her by name, and saying, "O thou, remember the Lord." Such

was the marriage of the blessed, and their perfect disposition toward those dearest to them.[8]

Peter practiced what he preached. The man who wrote, "Rejoice, though now for a little while, if necessary, you have been grieved by various trials" (verse 6), did indeed rejoice at the grievous sight of his own wife being led out to die. Keeping his eyes on Jesus kept Peter's eyes off the clock as it wound down toward their deaths. Peter and his wife learned from Jesus how to look at their crosses with joy and gladness. Peering inside Jesus's empty tomb gave Peter a new perspective about his own grave. Watching Jesus ascend to heaven gave him hope for the here and now. The exiles were finally returning home!

And Eusebius—you were so close! Why didn't you just tell us her name? Some people think St. Peter will greet us at the gates of heaven, and if that's true I hope his wife is standing right there beside him with the other unnamed women of the Bible like Peter's mother-in-law (Mark 1:30), the woman with the issue of blood (Mark 5:25–34), the widow with two coins (Mark 12:41–44), the Samaritan woman at the well (John 4:7–43), and the woman caught in adultery (John 8:3–11). Their names may escape us, but their stories have shaped us because even anonymous encounters with faith-filled women leave a lasting impression.

The pastor who spent ninety minutes teaching about the first three words in 1 Peter became a close friend to me and my entire family— in fact, I bake Ron and his wife, Marilyn, a cake each year on our Friendiversary. They have walked alongside me through many trials, encouraging and comforting me from the sidelines, shouting, "O Amy, remember the Lord!" Eusebius referred to this as the "perfect disposition" of our dearest disciple friends, Peter and his wife, toward one another and those around them, and it's the kind of discipling relationship I crave. Our fellow disciples don't deny or minimize our suffering; they don't help us plot and plan how to get out of it; they don't tell us we deserve better or it's going to be okay; and they don't promise that "God won't give you more than you can handle." True disciples remind us to remember the Lord as we carry our cross, even to our death. The strongest disciples stare their suffering right in the eye and boldly proclaim to everyone watching, "Watch me. I'll go first and show you how it's done."

As we remember the Lord, we will see God's grace in our suffering as Christ is revealed in his full glory. In 1 Peter 1, we've learned how to synchronize our hurting hearts with God's eternal clock to find joy and peace in the perplexing here and now:

> *Grace fully multiplied.*
> *Peace fully amplified.*
> *Faith fully tested, tried.*
> *Doubt fully gone, wiped.*
> *Mind fully calm and bright.*
> *Mercy fully brought to light.*
> *Joy fully, in our plight.*
> *Hope fully, just in Christ.*

A SECOND CUP

 Look up 2 Corinthians 12:7–10 to see that we're not alone when we ask God to give us what we want. What did God give Paul instead of the relief he craved? In verse 10, what does Paul say he is content with? When was the last time these strange items made it onto any list of things you are thankful for?

 Read a Hope Fully poem at www.amylively.com/hope -fully-poem or scan this code:

CAN I BORROW A CUP OF HOPE?

 Read 1 Peter 1 and draw a clock by verses with a reference to time, either past, present, or future.

Dear heavenly Father, when I'm faced with suffering, center my heart on you, fill my mind with your Word, and give me your grace to turn me to Christ. I trust your gifts, even when they come in strange packages. In Jesus's name, amen.

Lesson 5

Michelle's Story

Read 1 Peter 1:22–25

I MET MICHELLE THE FIRST time I entered a church on my own accord on a Sunday that wasn't a major religious holiday. Among an elderly congregation, this beautiful young woman leading worship stood out. Michelle fulfilled a need I didn't even know I had but Michelle shared. "I had been praying for several months for a friend who could walk through life with me, where I could be myself and we could pray and have devotions together," she remembers. God used her prayers to draw me back to himself, and then to her.

Over the years, we raised our children together and even helped plant a church together with our husbands and several other couples. Michelle has been my dearest friend and deepest mentor, she has discipled me and loved me; she has walked with me and even run with me (much to my objection). So many times, I've picked up the phone and called Michelle in desperation, yet she never tells me what I want to hear. She tells me what I need to hear. She is the kind of woman who will tell you chapter and verse what God's Word says about whatever you're facing.

Go get yourself a girlfriend like Michelle. You need her more than you know.

Music is an integral part of Michelle's life. As a young child she traveled the country with her father while he conducted revivals, and she sang with her sisters and their mother. "I remember crying because I didn't want to sing the high parts, but my mom would make me press through. Music ministers to me, and I like to use worship to help minister to others. I resort to music for comfort, singing words that echo what I find in the Bible."

When Michelle started a running group, she chose a verse to inspire her team because it spoke to both the physical and spiritual aspects of the sport:

> Therefore, since we are surrounded by such a huge crowd of witnesses to the life of faith, let us strip off every weight that slows us down, especially the sin that so easily trips us up. And let us run with endurance the race God has set before us. (Hebrews 12:1 NLT)

I always told Michelle if I ran into a tree during one of our early morning runs, it wasn't an accident—I was taking myself out of the race. Running is hard, so it makes sense that I've never met a Christian athlete who wasn't also steady and enduring in life and ministry. Michelle illustrates this in every way. "The disciplines we develop spiritually correlate with the way we train physically for an event. Running is not easy and it's not something you wake up every day eager to do," she admits. "But when the race starts, you're so glad you've done the training because you are able to finish."

Michelle's first date with her husband, Joe, was a five-kilometer race; their daughters, Kyleigh and Malauri, both ran competitively in high school and college. Joe also has a grown daughter who is raising her own beautiful family and a son who was killed in the line of duty as a police officer. A naturally gifted runner, Joe went on to complete several marathons, with a goal of qualifying for the Boston Marathon. "He was devastated when he was sidelined by an injury, and it was so hard to miss that opportunity." The year he missed qualifying turned out to be the year of the Boston Marathon bombing. "In hindsight, we could see God's hand working," Michelle recalls. "We could have been standing right there." The following year, at age sixty-five, Joe crossed the finish line in Boston as Michelle and their girls waved signs with their family motto, *Soli Deo Gloria*—glory to God alone.

A few months after Boston, Joe brought up vague and unrelated health complaints. There was nothing he could really put his finger on, but he wasn't feeling like his usual energetic self. Ongoing struggles with vertigo intensified, and he developed an inflammatory disorder that caused muscle pain and stiffness, especially in his shoulders and hips. "One morning he woke up and couldn't lift his arms, he couldn't get dressed, he couldn't get up from a chair," Michelle remembers. As a physical therapy assistant, Michelle knew this was unusual. "On his way to work one morning, he called me and said, 'I'm coming home. I'm itching from head to toe.'" He was diagnosed with a blockage in his bile duct, and a biopsy revealed the worst.

I'm speaking from experience when I tell you, if you google "bile duct cancer prognosis," it will suck the air right out of your lungs.

Joe endured extensive surgeries, chemotherapy, and radiation while Michelle worked full-time. They continued to travel to their daughters' college races around the country. He was seemingly doing well until his oncologist reported that his cancer marker numbers were on the rise. When faced with another round of treatment, Joe looked at Michelle and said, "I'm not going to do it again."

"I respected that, because I knew how much it took out of him," Michelle said. "Even though we were still able to travel, he didn't eat well; he was tired. He had painful side effects from the chemo. I knew it was diminishing the quality of his life, even though we did a really great job at *living*."

I saw Joe and Michelle in Florida in March 2020. Ever the caregiver, Michelle hovered with medications and pain relief, filling out complicated charts with each dosage and tracking all his meals. We caught a spring training baseball game and attended a triathlon where Malauri was competing, blissfully unaware of the lockdowns that would begin in just a few days. With all the strength he could muster, Joe stood and cheered as his daughter came out of the water, passed by on her bike, and ran across the finish line.

Back at the home they had rented, I sat beside Joe's wheelchair near the edge of the pool. "Joe, what is the Lord teaching you through all this?" I asked.

Wrapped in a sweatshirt with a blanket over his lap, his kind and gentle eyes closed against the sun, Joe replied, "Well you know, when I was first saved, I used to think it was great to pray once a day, and that was good enough. As I got older, I would pray more often and have more communion and fellowship with God. Now, I feel like I am with God always. I want to glorify God in what I'm going through."

I watched firsthand as Joe set his hope fully in the grace that would be given as Christ was revealed during his suffering. Joe ministered to his oncologist and later to the hospice staff, to his family at home and at church. He accepted whatever God was doing and was always able to convey his trust in God. Joe knew he wouldn't be able to fulfill so many of the things he dreamed he would do with his family. He cried, but he never complained. He didn't wallow in his suffering, but he did grieve. "I always told Joe this was the biggest race of his life, the most important finish line he would ever cross," Michelle said.

The pandemic was a strange gift as their family gathered at home with Kyleigh and Malauri during Joe's hospice care. "My biggest fear was knowing the right time to bring the girls home from college," Michelle recalls. "When the pandemic happened, I didn't have to worry about that anymore." Michelle's workplace also closed. The Lord encircled this precious family in their little log cabin in the woods of rural Ohio for six short weeks until Joe finished his race on May 6, 2020. When he drew his final breath, you may have heard the angels singing, "Well done, good and faithful servant!"

Later that morning, Michelle and all Joe's daughters shook a bottle of chilled champagne, popped the cork, and raised a toast to Joe's ultimate victory. "I kept the cork because I never want to forget what it felt like to celebrate something that really matters," Michelle said through her tears. "I also wanted to know that I celebrated something eternal with him."

Michelle's life motto became more real than she intended. "I didn't think *Soli Deo Gloria* would ever mean more than, 'Yay! We did it!' when we finished a race. Now I know what it really means.

"I was *hopeful* the treatments would work," she relays. "I was *hopeful* Joe would get into a clinical trial. I *hoped* he would still be here.

"You want to trust in modern medicine, you want to trust things you can try to control. I had to trust in the Lord with all my heart, without understanding what was happening, and acknowledge him in every one of the things that were far outside my control like it says in Proverbs 3:5–6. I had to believe God would continue to direct my life even when the world as I knew it ended. During the illness, Joe suffered most. Now I am suffering as I miss him and the normalcy and stability of the life we built. I know the one who carried me through Joe's death will carry me through the rest of my life."

Everyone who loved Joe watched him wither right before our eyes from a strong, able-bodied athlete to a shadow of the man he had once been physically—but spiritually, he was a giant. The closing words of the first chapter of 1 Peter exemplify how Joe lived, and how he died:

Having purified your souls by your obedience to the truth for a sincere brotherly love, love one another earnestly from a pure heart, since you have been born again, not of perishable seed but of imperishable, through the living and abiding word of God; for "All flesh is like grass and all its glory like the flower of grass. The grass withers, and the flower falls, but the word of the Lord remains forever." And this word is the good news that was preached to you. (1 Peter 1:22–25)

This Word was preached to Michelle in her childhood when she cried about the notes she didn't want to sing. The good news sustained her on long runs and races she didn't even sign up for. God used disappointment and disaster to train and equip her and Joe for a race they also didn't sign up for. Christ is her hope in life and death, in childhood and widowhood, in suffering and joy.

"God has been so faithful to me and has done things for me that only he could do," Michelle praises. "I have no doubt that I can fully trust him, and I hope fully in him."

A SECOND CUP ─────────────────────────

 As you read Michelle's story, you may have pictured your own "Joe" whose body faded away even as their spirit soared. Raise a toast and praise God for Joe or someone you love who exemplifies, "*Soli Deo Gloria!* Glory to God alone!"

 Who has come alongside you shouting, "O thou, remember the Lord!"? How did their encouragement change how you dealt with your challenges?

Who comes to mind that might need a reminder about God's faithfulness as they face a difficult time? Call that person or send them a note today letting them know you are cheering for them.

 Read 1 Peter 2–5 and pay special attention to verses about God's never-changing character and never-ending calendar. To remind you that our suffering will end in time, draw a clock beside any passage or phrase about a length of time or the past, present, or future.

Dear heavenly Father, thank you for your promise
that the suffering in this world doesn't last forever. When
this world feels overwhelming, please help my hope in
heaven sustain me through the hardest hours. I trust you,
no matter when or how you work in my life.
In Jesus's name, amen.

CHAPTER 2

JUST LIKE JESUS

1 Peter 2

With a ring burning a hole in his pocket, my boyfriend proposed while we were watching *Miami Vice* with my little brother. I remember how he wedged himself on one knee between the sofa and the coffee table, but there aren't any professional photos or viral videos capturing the special moment like you see today. Like every newly engaged woman still does, I found plenty of reasons to wave that sparkly ring around and admire it from varying angles.

The only time I haven't worn it was when I was pregnant and my fingers swelled (along with everything else), and even then I wore a plain gold band. I designed a new setting for the original diamond for our thirtieth anniversary and find myself admiring it all over again. It reminds me of the incredible man who chose me to be his bride and the choice we made to love each other as best we could. There aren't any pictures of the hard seasons or the not-so-pretty times, either, but each day we choose faithfulness, kindness, grace, and joy.

This is the theme of chapter 2 in 1 Peter, as Peter creates a picture of our life with Christ, who chose us to be his bride. When you read a verse about being chosen, called, or precious, draw a simple diamond ring beside it, something like this:

Jesus was also chosen and given a ceremonial symbol as a sign that he was specially selected by the Father. Yet Jesus suffered. There's an entire chapter in the Old Testament about "the Suffering Servant" that foretells the sad and sorrowful life of Christ (Isaiah 53—I can't wait to show you how it influences Peter's letter and our lives). Why did God allow Jesus to suffer? Why would he allow you to suffer? It's a legitimate question.

You have been chosen by God so that you may do his will . . . but what exactly is his will? Peter has planted clues throughout his letter that identify God's will and what he would like to accomplish through our everyday lives. Peter reaches back into Old Testament imagery to help us make sense of God's purposes and plans for our pain today. You'll also meet my dear friend Kelly and her family, who will show us how to carry a cup of hope in one hand and have the other raised in grateful praise.

 Scan this code or visit www.amylively.com/cup-of-hope /#chapter2 to access online resources and read the Scripture passages online.

Lesson 1

━ ✢ ━

The Chosen (St)One

Read Luke 20:9–20

ONE WINTER I SPENT WAY (way!) too much time bingeing the television series *Heartland*. On the show, a rite of passage for each member of the family is when a stone in the fireplace of the farmhouse they've lived in for generations is designated with their name. Together the stones make a strong tower (well, except for that one episode when Peter's parents come to visit) and represent a place of safety, warmth, and belonging.

This story resonates because we long to be included and accepted, we want to be part of something bigger than ourselves, and we want to know we're not alone. Let's look at how Jesus makes this possible.

Old Testament 1.0

Peter uses a lot of Old Testament references in this New Testament letter, especially in chapter 2, so hang tight while we do a quick and simple overview.

In the Old Testament, God revealed himself to a specific group of people called the Israelites, who were all descendants of a man named

Abraham. God promised Abraham he would have a huge family with as many descendants as the stars in the sky and that God would bless them all. God loved this family dearly and protected them fiercely, even during a long season when they were slaves to the Egyptians. He rescued them from Egypt, and after they wandered in the desert for forty years, God led them to a beautiful homeland of their own called the promised land.

God made strict laws to keep his people holy and safe, warning them not to mingle with other cultures who didn't follow his ways. God gave his people laws to govern all of life—from property rights and crime to cleanliness and worship rituals—in order to teach them how to live in relationship with God and one another. Their spiritual leaders were priests, men who all came from the same branch of the family tree. Priests were responsible for studying and teaching the law and interceding for the people when the law was broken.

The priests oversaw the temple in their capital city of Jerusalem. The temple was a beautiful, sacred building that represented God's home with humans. It was the hub of their religious and social lives. All Israelites were required to travel to the temple in Jerusalem several times a year for festivals and rituals. The people could gather in the courtyards around the temple, but only priests could enter the holy areas. A beautifully embroidered heavy curtain called a veil separated the holy places of the temple from the most holy place (creatively called the Most Holy Place), where God's presence was said to dwell. Early Jewish tradition said the veil was about sixty feet wide and thirty feet tall, as thick as a man's hand, and took three hundred priests to part![1] Only one priest was permitted to pass through the veil and enter the holiest part of the temple on just one day a year to atone for the sins of himself and the people, called the Day of Atonement.

And wow, were there a lot of sins. On the daily, the Israelites would touch something impure or do something unjust, violations of Scripture that made them unclean and unacceptable, and they would have to be quarantined so that they wouldn't pollute the entire population. The holy God could not wholly bless their unholiness. Because he loved them wholeheartedly, he made a way for them to come close to him again by permitting certain animals—inspected by the priests and found to be perfect, without any defects or blemishes—to be used as a payment to cover the penalty of their sin. The Israelites were reminded that sin results in death as the lifeblood of the animal slowly drained away, a vivid symbol of the consequence they deserved.

The Israelites turned from allegiance and obedience to rebellion and idolatry like a swinging door. One day they would sing God's praises and promise to obey his laws, and the next they'd be building altars to idols. God always sent messengers called prophets to deliver a message of warning, and he stood ready to welcome them back with open arms if they turned back to him. At times the Israelites were powerful, respected, and secure; they were always feared, hated, and attacked. Eventually, because of their ongoing sin, their kingdom fell to ruin, the temple was destroyed, and the people were taken away as captives. Some were permitted to return to Jerusalem, but it was never the same as it had once been. They prayed three times a day for someone to come restore their former glory (and they still do, to this very day).[2]

God promised to send this restorer, called the *Mashiach* (maw-shee-akh) in their language, or *Messiah* as we say in English. In Greek, the language the New Testament was written in, the word used for *Mashiach* is *Christos*, or *Christ* as we say in English. Whether you say *Mashiach* or *Messiah*, *Christos* or *Christ*, these words all mean "anointed," "the anointed one," or "the chosen one." Anointing was a ceremonial ritual where perfumed oil was smeared or poured on someone's head as a sign that they were chosen, or set apart, for a holy purpose. Kings, prophets, and priests were anointed, and sometimes special honored guests received this blessing. The temple building and sacred items used for worship and sacrifice were also anointed with oil.

The Jews had clues about the Messiah in their holy writings, the

Hebrew Bible (our Old Testament). Many thought he would be a national hero who would gather all the exiled people back to Jerusalem (Isaiah 11:12), rebuild their temple (Zechariah 6:12), bring perfect justice (Jeremiah 33:15), and usher in world peace (Micah 4:3). They were looking for a political leader and a spiritual giant, perfectly obedient to all their rules.

And they knew he would be a descendant of a king named David. Their endless genealogies, those long lists of "begats" that *some* people skip over in their Bible (you know who you are), helped them ensure that the Messiah could be tracked back to King David (Isaiah 11:1–9). The lists also identified who was eligible to receive the blessings God promised to Abraham's descendants.

While no one knew exactly when the Messiah would come, many understood he would arrive when either 1) Jewish persecution reached its peak or 2) they became perfectly obedient to all their rules and regulations.[3] With injustice and evil escalating all around them, it seemed hopeless that the Chosen One would come for God's chosen people any time soon.

New Testament 2.0

Enter Jesus. When a living, breathing, laughing, loving carpenter from a no-name village called Nazareth appeared on the scene and claimed to be the Messiah, many Jews found it hard to believe. He wasn't powerful enough to overtake the Romans who now ruled them, and he didn't play nicely with the religious leaders. He didn't keep their traditions about handwashing or avoiding moral derelicts or being still on the Sabbath day of rest. Sure, he seemed to know their holy writings pretty well, and he cast out demons and healed people of deadly diseases—but he claimed he could even forgive sins. Only God could do that! This didn't follow their preconceived Old Testament notions; it was an entirely new release, version 2.0—on steroids.

Jesus often taught in the temple in Jerusalem, which had taken forty-six years to rebuild. It was so awe-inspiring that his disciples once said to him, "Look, Teacher, what wonderful stones and what wonderful buildings!" Jesus, unimpressed, replied, "Do you see these great buildings? There will not be left here one stone upon another that will not be thrown down" (Mark 13:1–2). Jesus infuriated the religious leaders when he said, "Destroy this temple, and in three days I will raise it up" (John 2:19).

Jesus toppled the stones the Jews used to carefully construct their religious systems, and Peter had a front-row seat for the shake-up. He saw the outrage among the religious leaders as Jesus claimed to be the Messiah and was one of the first to believe Jesus was telling the truth. In Matthew 16:13–16, Jesus asked his followers who the Israelites thought he was. "Some say John the Baptist, others say Elijah, and others Jeremiah," they reported. When Jesus pressed them by asking, "But who do *you* say that I am?"—you, who have walked with me and camped with me, my closest friends and trusted confidants—it was Peter who proclaimed, "You are the Christ, the Son of the living God!" Jesus's last name is not Christ; Christ is his title, his identity, his anointing. Jesus is the Chosen One.

Jesus liked to teach in parables, simple stories with a spiritual twist. Peter was probably with Jesus when he told a parable to the chief priests in the temple about a man who planted a vineyard and leased it out to tenant farmers. The tenants repeatedly abused the man's messengers and finally killed his son, which led to their destruction (Luke 20:9–16). The religious leaders knew Jesus was talking about them, and they didn't miss the irony: they had been hatching a plot to attack Jesus just like the tenants in the parable. If the people hadn't been so infatuated with him, they would have done it right then! It was as if he knew their thoughts and schemes when Jesus looked directly at them and continued:

"What then is this that is written: 'The stone that the builders rejected has become the cornerstone'? Everyone who falls on that stone will be broken to pieces, and when it falls on anyone, it will crush him." (Luke 20:17–18)

The Chosen One is the chosen stone—the cornerstone, the firm foundation of our faith in God. Jesus combined two Old Testament passages to make this warning (Psalm 118:22 and Isaiah 8:14), and together they show how the Messiah, the long-awaited *Mashiach*, the crucial foundation for their faith, would be rejected as unfit and useless. His statement about rebuilding the temple in three days was twisted and used as evidence to crucify him, but he rose from the dead in three days after the temple of his body was destroyed—just like he promised. Jesus's perfect life, without defect or blemish, without sin or stain, qualified him to become a living sacrifice to atone for all sins, for all people, for all time. The bloody system of animal sacrifices ended once and for all, but that's not all he had in mind. Peter's words would soon rock the priesthood like nothing the priests had ever seen.

A SECOND CUP

What is your favorite binge-worthy show? I've watched fifteen seasons of *Heartland*, 234 episodes so far!

Read Romans 5:6–8. What time was it when Christ died for us (verse 6)? What were we doing (verse 8)? If our behavior determined when the *Mashiach* would come, what would the state of the world be today?

The Israelites are an example to Christians today because they were a people who were chosen and treasured by God, even when their obedience, faith, and trust wavered. In what ways do you relate to the Israelites?

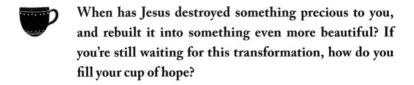 **When has Jesus destroyed something precious to you, and rebuilt it into something even more beautiful? If you're still waiting for this transformation, how do you fill your cup of hope?**

Compare Matthew 7:24–25 with Matthew 16:18. How did Jesus follow his own advice when building his church? What is the future of the kingdom of God based on in these passages?

Read 1 Peter 2 in your Bible and draw a diamond ring like this one beside verses that mention being chosen, called, elected, precious, and so on.

Dear heavenly Father, thank you for sending your Son when we needed you most. My heart rejoices because you are the perfect and spotless lamb who takes away the sins of the world—especially mine. You alone are the cornerstone and solid foundation upon which I will build my life. In Jesus's name, amen.

Lesson 2

~ ❖ ~

Living Stones

Read Acts 4:1–12 and 1 Peter 2:1–9

LATER IN PETER'S LIFE, HE was rejected, attacked, and arrested because of his belief in the resurrected Jesus. In a scene remarkably similar to Luke 20:17, Peter boldly proclaimed the same words Jesus spoke to the high priest, religious rulers, leaders, and legal experts when they disputed him. Peter, filled with the Holy Spirit, said to his accusers:

> "Jesus is the stone that was rejected by you, the builders, which has become the cornerstone. And there is salvation in no one else, for there is no other name under heaven given among men by which we must be saved." (Acts 4:11–12)

I think these were some of Peter's favorites of Jesus's words because of the special title Jesus gave him: *Petros*, or the rock. "See what I did there?" I imagine Peter saying. "Jesus is the cornerstone, he called me the rock . . . Get it?" Peter cited these verses again in 1 Peter 2, when he referred to Jesus by a new sort of title.

As you come to him, a living stone rejected by men but in the sight of God chosen and precious, you yourselves like living stones are being built up as a spiritual house, to be a holy priesthood, to offer spiritual sacrifices acceptable to God through Jesus Christ. For it stands in Scripture: "Behold, I am laying in Zion a stone, a cornerstone chosen and precious, and whoever believes in him will not be put to shame." So the honor is for you who believe, but for those who do not believe, "The stone that the builders rejected has become the cornerstone," and "A stone of stumbling, and a rock of offense." (1 Peter 2:4–8)

When you think about it, we can add "living stone" to the list of oxymorons discussed earlier, because how can an inert stone have life and breath? Stones are about the least "living" things imaginable: they're cold and hard, and in the Rocky Mountains where I live, they're enormous and even deadly. Every September, my small community pauses to remember a family who perished in a devastating rockslide.

Stones can come crashing down, but they can also be essential for building things up. The first step in erecting the temple, and every other stone building you've ever seen, is to position a cornerstone, which determines the stability and stamina of the entire structure. Jesus is the cornerstone of his church, and Peter one of the first stones to be stacked upon him. You and I are stones that build up the church, undergirded by the saints who came before us, laid side by side with those who worship and work with us, and supportive of the ones who come after us. The church is a collection of carefully chosen living stones mortared together by the love of Christ.

Peter witnessed how Jesus, the cornerstone, was "rejected by men" but "chosen and precious"—and you, dear one, are just like Jesus. Jesus was chosen and anointed, appointed and selected for the work God planned for him to do. He was also disregarded, hunted, threatened, tested, betrayed, scorned, mocked, and murdered before he was resurrected and restored.

Just like Jesus, we will be scorned. Just like Jesus, we will suffer now before we have glory later. And just like Jesus, we are chosen by God for his specific purposes. What, then, are God's purposes in our sorrow and our suffering? Why did he choose you?

Chosen to Scatter

The Israelites were familiar with what it meant to be scattered. They spent a large part of their early history wandering aimlessly, not willing and then not able to enter the promised land. They even had a name for when they were taken captive and hauled away from their homeland by foreign nations: the Diaspora. So when Peter wrote this letter to the "elect exiles of the Dispersion," they knew exactly what he meant, even though Peter was addressing first-century Christians scattered across the Roman Empire rather than ancient Israelites. Jesus also knew what it was like to live as an exile. His parents were forced to flee from Bethlehem, where he was born, to the neighboring country of Egypt. Jesus traveled throughout Judea and Samaria and stayed in the homes of his followers but had no place he called his own (Matthew 8:20). He willingly left his home in heaven to walk in our dust, until he was buried in our dirt.

As Jesus's followers, we are also exiles who look out the window and ask, "Where are we?" Lots of us may be utterly perplexed by the "new normal" we awaken to in the morning, still exhausted from yesterday's changes and challenges. We may feel like strangers in our own homes, an exile in our own minds, outcasts in a culture that's morphed into something unrecognizable. Spiritually, we long to be fully united with Christ, which we can't experience on this side of heaven. Culturally, we see others in our community practicing strange customs that go against our beliefs. But geographically, just like Jesus and the Israelites, we have been carefully placed in our neighborhoods to bless the people living around us.

> Build houses and settle down; plant gardens and eat what they produce. . . . Also, seek the peace and prosperity of the city to which I have carried you into exile. Pray to the LORD for it, because if it prospers, you too will prosper. (Jeremiah 29:5, 7 NIV)

When we want to run away, he asks us to stay, to play, to pray. At work, where break room stories break your heart. At the park where your children play while you pray with other moms. On the golf course or at the clubhouse, where small talk can lead to deep conversation. Perhaps even in your own home, where you may be the only citizen of heaven in a family of lost souls. Where we're scattered matters, because God has arranged for us to meet other weary travelers waiting to be welcomed home. Just like Jesus, your exile is intentional, and God has chosen you to be in a specific place for his purposes.

Chosen to Serve

Another reason God chooses us is so that we can serve as priests. Wait a minute, wait a minute! Priests in Peter's day were born into their roles. A person couldn't be a priest unless he was a Jewish man from a specific family. Women or non-Jews need not apply. The role of a priest was clearly defined and the rituals strictly enforced. Only the priest could offer atoning sacrifices, have access to the holy writings, and act as the people's representative to God. God widening the playing field for who could be a priest was a game changer.

> You yourselves like living stones are being built up as a spiritual house, *to be a holy priesthood.* (1 Peter 2:5)

Peter anoints women and men, Jews and non-Jews, young and old, from every nation, every tribe, every language as priests! So are we supposed to work at church or slaughter animals all day? No, thank you—this is so much better! Old Testament priests were the only ones qualified to enter the temple's holy places; as New Testament priests, we *are* the holy place—the sacred building has become a sacred body, and the Spirit of Christ dwells in our hearts. Instead of causing the bloodshed of animals, we are covered by the blood of Christ. Instead of obeying legalistic rules, we have an all-access grace pass. Instead of walking to Jerusalem, we walk beside Jesus. God's Word is written in our hearts, and he helps us understand.

The invitation to serve as a priest is a calling into the presence of God, being chosen for service in his kingdom, specially selected to witness his glory. We are anointed not by a vial of perfumed oil but by the sweetness of the Holy Spirit, who marks us as holy, sacred, and chosen.

Chosen to Sacrifice

We are also chosen to offer sacrifices to God. Gosh, that sounds like just as much fun as being a priest!

> You yourselves like living stones are being built up as a spiritual house . . . *to offer spiritual sacrifices* acceptable to God through Jesus Christ. (1 Peter 2:5)

The Old Testament is full of gory scenes of slaughter and the splashing blood of animals that were killed to compensate or atone for sins. Now that Christ has paid for our sins, once and for all, with the shedding of his precious blood on the cross, the only sacrifices needed are of the spiritual nature . . . which may hurt even worse. To offer a spiritual sacrifice is to give something of yourself to honor God. Spiritual sacrifices include praising God in good times and bad, doing good deeds, sharing with others, and returning to God the financial gifts he's given to you. We'll explore these in "A Second Cup."

Jesus told Peter and the disciples what a life of spiritual sacrifice would look like.

> "If anyone would come after me, let him deny himself and take up his cross and follow me. For whoever would save his life will lose it, but whoever loses his life for my sake will find it." (Matthew 16:24–25)

To deny oneself is to lay our self and our "self-sins" on the altar—"self-righteousness, self-pity, self-confidence, self-sufficiency, self-admiration, and self-love," according to A. W. Tozer[4]—as well as all the newfangled distractions like self-actualization, self-care, self-awareness, self-esteem, and self-gratification. Ouch! It hurts to let God cut away our self-centeredness until we are completely centered in his will.

Taking up our cross means following Jesus's footsteps to our own Golgotha, the "Place of a Skull," where he was crucified (Matthew 27:33). At the same time as religious leaders sacrificed perfect, unblemished lambs during their Passover ritual, Jesus—the spotless Lamb of God—willingly sacrificed his life for our sake. In the same text, Tozer wrote, "It is never fun to die. To rip through the dear and tender stuff of which life is made can never be anything but deeply painful. Yet that is what the cross did to Jesus"—and that is what picking up your cross will do to you.

It is never fun to die to ourselves. It hurts to sacrifice our selfish hearts, and it is deeply painful to give up our rights for the sake of others. Yet here we find a truth we won't learn in any self-help book: when you lay your soul on the altar as a spiritual sacrifice, Christ will resurrect you to your best life ever.

A SECOND CUP

 Read Jeremiah 29:1–14. Where are the people of Judah in this passage (verse 1)? What are they told to do (verses 5–7)? What can we do while we wait for God to rescue us (verse 12)? Verse 11 is a perennial favorite. How does the context surrounding verse 11 surprise you or change your understanding? During our spiritual exile, what promises does God make (verses 10, 14)? What reassurance does that give you during your journey?

 Review the responsibilities of the Old Testament priest from Lesson 1. How do we, as modern-day believers, live out these roles in our own hearts and homes now that Peter has called us to be "a holy priesthood"?

 Read Hebrews 4:16 and 10:19–22. As a New Testament believer, what can you do anytime that Old Testament priests could only do once a year? How could you take advantage of this privilege in a more meaningful way?

 In 1 Peter 2:5, Peter says we are to offer ourselves as spiritual sacrifices, giving something of ourselves to honor God. According to the verses below, what can we give as a spiritual sacrifice?

> Romans 12:1–3
> Philippians 4:18
> Hebrews 13:15
> Hebrews 13:16
> Revelation 8:3–4

*Dear heavenly Father, it's beyond my comprehension that
you have chosen me to serve in your kingdom. Remind me
of my duties and privileges as your treasured possession,
and draw me into the Most Holy Place of your presence.
Help me to gladly offer everything I have to you.
In Jesus's name, amen.*

Lesson 3

~ ❊ ~

The Stones Cry Out

Read 1 Peter 2:9–15, 20–21; 3:9; 5:10

THERE'S NOTHING QUITE LIKE SUFFERING to teach us about Jesus. When we follow his footsteps, pain that would slay us becomes prayer that revives us, and stones hurled by tormentors become jewels in our crowns. Peter would never ask us to do anything that Jesus hasn't already done. We can look to Jesus's example to find God's higher calling and greater purpose in choosing us. Let's continue looking at what we are chosen for as Christ followers.

Chosen to Speak

The next reason we are chosen is to speak, or as Peter more eloquently stated it,

> But you are a *chosen* race, a royal priesthood, a holy nation, a people for his own possession, *that you may proclaim* the excellencies of him who called you out of darkness into his marvelous light. (1 Peter 2:9)

We're not chosen so we can sit prettily and bask in our loveliness until we're whisked off to heaven. We are called so that we can call others. When God transforms your sorrow into joy, your suffering into glory, and your sin into salvation, you've gotta tell somebody! Our stories are for his glory, and they need to be shouted from the mountaintops. If we, as living stones, don't speak his praise, Jesus said that even the stones of the ground would cry out (Luke 19:40)!

Chosen to Silence

It's almost like Peter foresaw today's hostile culture when he wrote the next reason we are chosen.

> For *this is the will of God*, that by doing good you should put to *silence* the ignorance of foolish people. (1 Peter 2:15)

There will always be those who try to discredit the testimony of people who claim to be Christians. They delight in smashing the pedestals they believe we've placed ourselves on and take great joy when we fail to live up to our own standards. But our testimonies are necessary, because it's God's will that we do good in obvious and overt ways that will silence ignorant and unknowledgeable people. A life of integrity is the best defense against false accusations.

But since we're broken people living in a fallen world, there's a good chance we'll give others plenty of ammunition and opportunity to criticize our claims and attempt to cancel our testimonies. We aren't perfect, but we can be perfectly humble and honest when we falter. We can confess our mistakes, ask for forgiveness, and accept the consequences.

There will be times when doing good means accepting bad circumstances—just like Jesus did. His silence before his accusers silenced their accusations. We can't underestimate the message we send when we set aside our rights and freedoms for the benefit of others. We are chosen so that we can lead exemplary lives among lost people, pointing to the prime example of Jesus Christ.

Chosen to Sustain

Peter provided us with a perfect example to follow on our chosen road.

> For what credit is it if, when you sin and are beaten for it, you endure? But if when you do good and suffer for it you *endure*, this is a gracious thing in the sight of God. For *to this you have been called*, because Christ also suffered for you, leaving you an example, so that you might *follow in his steps*. (1 Peter 2:20–21)

When we place our feet where Jesus has already walked, we're on pace for an epic race. Endurance athletes do 3,000-mile bike rides, jog across 150-mile deserts carrying their food and water on their backs, or trek 1,000 miles across the Alaskan tundra in winter. Ironman triathletes swim 2.4 miles followed by biking 112 miles, with a 26.2-mile marathon as a cooldown. My husband has done this *twice*. On purpose! The training, stamina, and perseverance are incredible to watch.

When we bravely and patiently endure suffering without dropping out of the race, the prize is grace. When you're belittled by people who say your faith leaves your brain behind, when you're teased if you talk about God, and when your good works get you a bad rap, then you are truly suffering for Jesus. Around the world, Christians are brutalized and murdered because of their faith in Jesus—yet they refuse to deny his name. Saints are entrusted with suffering because their testimony under duress brings glory to God as they bear up and endure by his grace. When you set your hope fully on the prize of grace, it's placed around your neck like a medal when you cross the finish line.

Please note that suffering for being a jerk doesn't count; Peter is specifically referring to suffering because of your faith in Christ. Christians should be the hardest workers, kindest neighbors, biggest tippers at lunch after church, fastest to return their shopping cart to the carousel, liveliest volunteers, and most upstanding members of community, so that our testimonies aren't tarnished.

Chosen to Smile

We are chosen to smile upon the difficult people around us.

> Do not repay evil for evil or reviling for reviling, but on the contrary, *bless*, for *to this you were called*, that you may obtain a blessing. (1 Peter 3:9)

Could it be that the really mean coworker, the nasty neighbor, the snarky in-law, and the challenging child are intentionally put in our paths just so that we can bless them? This one is hard for me. When someone hurts me, I want to hurt them right back—and fast! When I've been wronged, I want to make it right—on my terms. When I'm not getting my own way, I want to be a bulldozer. In a battle of words, I want the last one.

Peter tells us to do the exact opposite. We have been placed in proximity to prickly people at this time for this purpose of blessing them—asking God to give them his very best, praying for their prosperity and their salvation. Who else is going to bless such a scoundrel?

As my father taught me when someone hurt me badly, "Asking God to bless someone doesn't mean you want sugar and spice and everything nice for them." He explained, "God's best blessing comes when we walk in his ways, and he'll do whatever it takes to turn a person's heart." When we bless someone who has hurt us, we are trusting God to deal with the evil in their lives instead of trying to correct or punish it ourselves. God sees what they did, but he rewards what you do. You have been chosen, called, and equipped for this.

Chosen to Share

As we've already covered a bit already, no one understands spiritual transformation quite like Peter, who failed his tests before finally passing with flying colors. Peter was beautifully restored to Christ personally, among his peers, and in his community. Peter brought some of his suffering upon himself as he bungled his way through the events of the Bible, but Jesus never gave up on him. Peter ended his ministry secure in the knowledge that he was a partaker, a partner, and a sharer in God's glory. He referred to himself as:

> A witness of the sufferings of Christ, as well as a *partaker in the glory* that is going to be revealed. (1 Peter 5:1)

Peter extended this invitation to us as well:

> But rejoice insofar as *you share Christ's sufferings*, that you may also rejoice and be glad when his glory is revealed. (1 Peter 4:13)

All glory belongs to God alone, but he invites us to share and experience it with him as we pick up our cross and follow Jesus. He shares the Spirit of glory (1 Peter 4:14) by sending him to dwell within us—not beside us, not behind us, not before us, but inside us. Peter concluded his own story like this:

> And after you have suffered a little while, the God of all grace, who has *called* you to his eternal glory in Christ, will himself restore, confirm, strengthen, and establish you. (1 Peter 5:10)

God has chosen and called you to step into the presence of his eternal glory. After suffering comes strength and restoration. After a hard little while comes a heavenly eternity. When we surrender our suffering into Jesus's nail-scarred hands, he gives us back grace and glory.

A SECOND CUP

 Do you agree or disagree with the statement, "We are called so that we can call others"? Consider Paul's recounting of his own testimony in Acts 26:16–18 as you answer.

 What is the outcome of suffering according to Romans 5:3–5 and James 1:2–4? Why do these verses indicate that our suffering causes joy?

 How have you felt Christ restore, confirm, strengthen, and establish you after a season of suffering?

Dear heavenly Father, I trust you with my suffering. Help me to be strong until it ends so that I may share your glory. In my pain, may I proclaim your goodness and grace. In Jesus's name, amen.

Lesson 4

~ ❖ ~

And Chosen to Suffer

Read 1 Peter 2:21–25; 4:13

WHEN PETER WAS FOURTEEN OR fifteen years old, he would have been questioned by the rabbis, the Jewish scholars or teachers who were appointed as religious leaders. They looked for young men to follow them and become their disciples, a concept that was well understood in Jewish culture long before Jesus made the words familiar to us. But because Peter and his friends James and John were partners in a fishing business (Luke 5:10), we know that Peter must have been rejected by his local rabbis as unqualified, unwanted, and incapable of being their disciple. They would have told him, "Go home and ply your trade."[5] Being a fisherman was a second-best life.

Peter was soaking wet when he met Jesus, casting his nets into the Sea of Galilee with his brother, Andrew. Jesus's first words to Peter were, "Follow me" (Mark 1:17), and Peter dropped everything to do just that. He swapped fishing for the daily catch to fishing for eternal souls. When he wasn't hosting Jesus in his own home, our waterlogged boater found himself hiking the dry, dusty roads throughout Judea and Samaria. The ancient blessing he'd heard all his life was finally coming true: "Let thy house be a meeting-house for the wise; and powder thyself in the dust of their feet; and drink their words with thirstiness."[6]

Peter was chosen for more than just formal education and a new kind of fishing. He was chosen for suffering. He would follow Jesus falteringly at first, until ultimately, he would follow him all the way to his own cross. Watching his rabbi suffer gave Peter the strength to place his sandals in the dusty imprints left by his friend on the path to his own crucifixion.

For *to this you have been called*, because Christ also suffered for you, leaving you an example, so that you might *follow in his steps*. (1 Peter 2:21)

The word Peter used for *example* is found only once in the Bible (for you word geeks like me, this is called *hapax legomena*, or "once spoken"). The compound word *hypogrammos* (hoop-og-ram-*mos*) means "under writing," and it was a template given to beginning pupils so they could make an exact replica of the alphabet by tracing over the letters. Recalling Christ's final hours and his crucifixion, Peter retraced Jesus's steps and laid that unforgettable day over a passage from Isaiah he most likely learned as a young student:

1 Peter 2	Isaiah 53
[22] He committed no sin, neither was deceit found in his mouth.	[9] he had done no violence, and there was no deceit in his mouth.
[23] When he was reviled, he did not revile in return; when he suffered, he did not threaten, but continued entrusting himself to him who judges justly.	[7] He was oppressed, and he was afflicted, yet he opened not his mouth; like a lamb that is led to the slaughter, and like a sheep that before its shearers is silent, so he opened not his mouth.

1 Peter 2	Isaiah 53
[24] He himself bore our sins in his body on the tree,	[4] Surely he has borne our griefs and carried our sorrows [11] he shall bear their iniquities. [12] he bore the sin of many, and makes intercession for the transgressors.
that we might die to sin and live to righteousness.	[11] by his knowledge shall the righteous one, my servant, make many to be accounted righteous,
By his wounds you have been healed.	[5] with his wounds we are healed.
[25] For you were straying like sheep, but have now returned to the Shepherd and Overseer of your souls.	[6] All we like sheep have gone astray; we have turned—every one—to his own way.

The scroll Peter had heard his rabbis read aloud in the synagogue near his home came to life before his eyes, and now he could not take his eyes off Jesus.

Peter didn't learn his Christology (the branch of Christian theology that relates to the person, nature, and role of Christ) in a classroom—he learned it at the cross. He had hugged Jesus and sat with him around a fire. They had laughed and argued together. They knew each other's families.

If you really want to know Jesus like Peter knew Jesus, seek him when you suffer unjustly. Just like they did Jesus, people will persecute you, say untrue things about you, and plan evil to harm you. You will be ostracized, ignored, scorned, and scoffed at. But as biblical scholar Karen Jobes notes, this is "not evidence that God has forsaken you; to the contrary, it is evidence that God has chosen you."[7] Instead of having us cower in fear or retaliate in anger, Jesus helps us rest in the reward we know we'll receive after the agony.

> But rejoice insofar as you share Christ's sufferings, that you may also rejoice and be glad when his glory is revealed. (1 Peter 4:13)

Forever Chosen

I don't usually speak King James, but for some reason I wanted to say, "With this ring, I thee wed," during my vows. Ever since, the fourth finger of my left hand has a permanent indentation from wearing my wedding ring for well over thirty years, a public proclamation of love and faithfulness.

Modern Greeks use the word *arravónas* (ar-hrah-*vohn*-as) to refer to their engagements.[8] Couples exchange simple gold bands engraved with the bride's and groom's name and their upcoming wedding date. The rings are traditionally blessed by a priest and placed on their left hands until the wedding, when they are moved to the right hand.[9] In the New Testament, the same root word, *arrabōn* (ar-hrab-*ohn*), is used to describe the pledge or guarantee of the Holy Spirit given to all who believe (more on this in "A Second Cup").

Like a starry-eyed lover with a ring burning a hole in his pocket, God has placed the Holy Spirit in your heart as a lasting sign that you are forever chosen. He will stay by your side when you are scattered. He will help you serve in holiness and receive the costly sacrifices you offer of yourself. He'll give you words to speak and the strength to silence your accusers. He will hold your hand to sustain you through hard times and turn your lips to smile upon those who wish you harm.

He will share with you a crown of grace and the gift of glory. Your Father looks down from heaven and reaches his hand toward you as he declares, "Her. I choose her. She is precious and she's mine."

A SECOND CUP

As you reflect upon your walk with Christ, can you identify seasons when he has chosen you to: Scatter to a dark place that needs his light? Serve as a priest in his presence? Sacrifice something of yourself? Speak his praise? Sustain through a long, difficult season? Smile upon someone who has hurt you? Share his suffering as well as his glory?

The Greek word *arrabōn* is interpreted as guarantee, pledge, or down payment in various Bible translations. Modern Greeks use this root word to refer to their engagements with the exchanging of rings. What has God given believers as his guarantee in the following verses?

2 Corinthians 1:22
2 Corinthians 5:5
Ephesians 1:13–14

What has been guaranteed in Ephesians 1:14? How does this guarantee encourage you?

Read Isaiah 41:8–13.
Because God has chosen you, what will he never do (verse 9)? Which of his hands does God use to hold you (verse 10)?

Which of your hands is God holding (verse 13)?
Wear a ring or bracelet on your right hand to remind you
of God's promise, "Fear not, I am the one who helps you"
(verse 13).

Dear heavenly Father, thank you for sending your Son to
be the Shepherd and Overseer of my soul. Thank you for
giving me your Spirit as a guarantee of my eternal life
with you. Help me to live secure in the promise that you
will never leave me, even when I am suffering.
In Jesus's name, amen.

Lesson 5

⁓ ✳ ⁓

Kelly's Story

Read 1 Peter 2:17

Buena Vista, Colorado—or BV, as the locals call it—holds special significance to Kelly Fohner and her family. Kelly had the best week of her life at the Frontier Ranch Young Life camp in BV when she was a junior in high school. It was a turning point in her faith, so she was thrilled to accompany her husband, Mike, to minister at Frontier Ranch and nearby Trail West when he worked for Young Life. They still return to vacation locally with their three children.

Their middle son, Josh, joined the Navy right out of college. While training to become a Navy SEAL, he suffered a severe shoulder injury that eventually led to a medical discharge. This was Josh's first TEOT-WAWKI moment, the end of his dream to serve in the special forces. He had been recovering and figuring out a new course for his life for about a year when he broached the idea of moving to Buena Vista in July 2016. Kelly was thrilled and encouraged him to go. "I wish I could go with you!" she said.

Josh settled quickly into the one-traffic-light town he'd visited all his life, working a couple of part-time jobs and easily making friends.

The day after a festive community dinner called BV Strong, the always-disciplined Josh woke up early and rode his bicycle to the gym before work. It would be the last time Josh would go anywhere he wanted to go and do whatever he wanted to do before TEOTWAWKI #2, when he was struck by a Jeep on the ride home.

Back home in Arkansas, Mike ignored repeated phone calls during a business meeting until he noticed the caller ID. When he returned the call, a nurse on the other end of the line said, "We think we have your son." Police attending the accident scene had retained Josh's wallet, so the hospital listed him as "Paramount Doe." A bear claw tattoo on Josh's chest confirmed his identity and brought Mike's world crashing down.

Kelly was summoned to the principal's office at the school where she taught, something that strikes fear even into adult hearts. Her TEOTWAWKI moment came as Mike explained that Josh had been in an accident and was unresponsive. "Let's go!" she declared, and they made a fifteen-minute stop at their home to pack a bag before turning their car west for the eight-hundred-mile journey.

They would not return for seven months.

They were greeted at the hospital by a huge crowd of friends, family, and pastors, all praying for a miracle. The neurosurgeon who had been attending to Josh stayed until they arrived in the middle of the night. The pictures on his screen showed a severe brain injury, a broken neck, a fractured back, and multiple facial fractures. The prognosis was bleak, and Kelly and Mike struggled to sift through what was real and what was merely speculative.

In the first three days after the accident, the family clung to three specific comforts. The first was a verse they posted all over Josh's hospital room:

Now all glory to God, who is able, through his mighty power at work within us, to accomplish infinitely more than we might ask or think. (Ephesians 3:20 NLT)

The second was the word *gratitude* as they were overwhelmed with the amount of support and the ways they saw God's provision after the accident.

The third was the promise given by the BV chief of police: "God's got this!" Chief Jimmy Tidwell told them that the first people on the scene were a former Special Ops medic, a pharmacist, and a Young Life camp manager who were jogging about fifty yards away. Prayers rose the instant Josh's body fell. Only an experienced medic would have dared touch Josh's broken body, but this man knew what to do. A Life Flight helicopter stood at the ready to fly Josh to Colorado Springs after being stationed in BV overnight after the community dinner. All the pieces were in place to handle this crisis.

Josh was also well trained and spiritually prepared for what he was about to face. In typical all-or-nothing Josh fashion, he had never looked back after becoming a Christian. "Coming home from a church mission trip, he walked right off that bus, came straight up to me and said, 'I made a commitment to Christ,'" Kelly smiles. Josh had a heart for serving the unserved, although free meals and pretty girls were nice perks when he served as a houseboy at a sorority in college. Once a sorority member asked him what he was studying, but he was reading his Bible. "I'm memorizing Scripture," he told her, "because I don't want to be without this Word if there's ever a time when I can't read it." Josh's life verse is from 1 Peter 2.

> Honor everyone. Love the brotherhood. Fear God. Honor the emperor. (1 Peter 2:17)

Although his accident happened less than a mile from my Colorado home, I met Josh, Kelly, and Mike for the first time when travels brought me near the hospital where Josh was being treated in Texas. He had been transferred to the San Antonio Polytrauma Rehabilitation Center, one of five facilities in the country designed to provide intensive rehabilitative care to veterans and service members who have experienced severe brain injuries. Because his previous injury from special operations training was considered a combat injury, Josh had access to the best physicians, therapy, and equipment after his brain injury. Mike and Kelly received free housing during their long stay by Josh's side. Josh's brief military service, which hadn't ended the way he envisioned, ended up being an essential component of his care.

"At first, we just prayed that Josh would live," Kelly remembers. But in their secret dreams they hoped for the Hollywood ending. "We hoped Josh would wake up from his coma and everything would be fine, and he'd be able to put his life back together incredibly fast, just like the movies." It became evident in a short amount of time that there would be no quick fixes, as Josh remained in a coma for fifteen months.

"We had to make a choice," Kelly says. "We could either hope fully in God, or we could collapse. Trusting God at that point was not the easy choice, but for us it was the only choice." In a large medical center, there aren't many quiet places to get away and be alone, so a hard cement bench near the intersection of the hospital parking garage, a Chick-fil-A, and a Starbucks became Kelly's sanctuary. "Lord, thank you for where we are," she prayed, continually going to that place of gratitude. "You have provided for us, you have cared for us and carried us."

Cards, text messages, and emails poured in from around the world, and Josh's family transcribed them onto brightly colored sticky notes that were plastered around his room along with pictures of Josh (in every one, he's either making a funny face or standing beside a pretty girl). "We needed the people who were caring for Josh to see him as a person, not just a patient. It was interesting to watch the dynamics change as the medical personnel picked out their favorite pictures," Kelly recalls. "The neurosurgeon shared that he also served with special operations in the Navy after he saw Josh's photos. They opened themselves up to us as they saw Josh as a person, not just an injury."

In the years since the accident, Josh has made incredible progress.

"We watched his doctors go from *maybe* to *if* to *when*," Kelly states proudly. "Josh has made a believer out of everybody." At a recent return visit to San Antonio, his surgeon said, "I have never seen a patient with his level of injury still improving so many years postaccident and with this much function."

Although trapped inside a body he's trying to make work again, Josh is fully cognitive. He communicates by spelling with his foot, tapping out letters. "Everyone who comes into contact with him knows he's all there; it's not just Mom and Dad saying that," Mike brags. He texts with his friends and family more regularly than a teenager with his first cell phone. He cannot speak, but Kelly says, "He knows those things are coming, and he continues to learn sounds." Josh has made great strides in defying expectations. For example, Josh (the guy who can't speak!) was asked to share his story with a communications class at his alma mater, the University of Arkansas. Additionally, as an avid outdoorsman, Josh has been skiing and waterskiing since the accident at the National Ability Center in Park City, Utah. He's able to operate his wheelchair using head and knee switches.

Five years after Mike and Kelly packed their car and hurried west, Josh led them home on a 908-mile cross-country bike trek. Over 150 bicyclists joined them for different parts of the ride, and Josh pedaled every single mile on his specially adapted recumbent tandem bike. The quad strength Josh gained from his training regime has since enabled him to stand on his own, and he is beginning to take assisted steps. As you pray for Josh, his big dreams now are talking, walking, and eating—in that order. You can follow his journey at www.amylively.com/josh or scan this code:

I ask Kelly's family what they have seen in her over the past several years. Mike lovingly shares, "From the very first day, everything we knew was gone. We were alone and powerless. Every moment was a prayer. Kelly knew only God could help us. Kelly clung to her faith and trust in him. She learned how to find joy in the Lord and therefore joy in our circumstance. He was her strength."

Their oldest son, John Michael, has learned from his mom's constancy. "She is constant in her faith, constant in her attitude, constant in her love. She accepts the situation, she deals with it, and she looks for ways to bring joy. She told us, 'We will do whatever we need to do, and that will be the end of it.' She doesn't dwell on the past and is thankful for what we have been given."

Daughter Maggie has never felt a change in the way Kelly cares for her and loves her since the accident. "It's easy for me to feel selfish for needing my mom when she is giving so much taking care of Josh, but Mom has only expanded the ways she shows up for me. She is so in tune with each of us, and meets us where we are, even when we don't realize that's exactly what we need."

Alex, Josh's BV roommate, will never forget talking with Kelly in the hospital after the accident. "The first thing that came out of Kelly's mouth was, 'Please let the individual who hit Josh know that we forgive him!' I'm so thankful I've been able to witness this and be a part of it." (By the way, Alex is no longer just a roommate, he's a brother—he married Josh's sister!)

Josh taps out a message about his mom. "I am always thankful she is willing to set her life, her hopes, and her future aside so I might have a life, a hope, and a future. This gives me great joy."

"When you cling to gratitude, it changes you and everyone around you," Kelly says. "A picture that kept coming to my mind was someone sinking in quicksand, like I saw on Saturday morning cartoons when I was a child. Whenever gratitude slipped away, it felt like struggling in quicksand, sinking lower and lower. Gratitude was a hand that reached out and helped me hold on. Gratitude always took me back to a place of hope, and that leads to contentment."

"Hope does incredible things," Kelly says admiringly of Josh. "He knows he's going to be fine; he tells me that all the time. Hope looks unique to the people who are watching; it stands out. When you're hopeful and have a heart of gratitude, it's contagious."

"God has equipped Josh to handle this," Kelly attests. "We trust that. I no longer have a list of things I want or am hopeful will happen. My prayers are focused on gratitude, which gives me hope."

For every hopeless TEOTWAWKI moment the Fohners faced, there was a hope-full "God's got this!" right behind it. Kelly laughs without fear of the future. "Uncertainty does not scare me anymore."

The Fohners were *scattered* from their home and thus had countless opportunities to share the hope that they have with other devastated families and weary medical staff. Josh continues to *serve* God and bless others with his uncomplaining attitude in unimaginable crisis. With one voice, their family offers the spiritual *sacrifice* of praise and lays down their needs to meet the needs of others. They have *spoken* and shouted God's praises from the mountaintops that overlooked the scene of Josh's accident! Skeptics have been *silenced* as they've seen firsthand God's mighty hand knitting Josh's body back together, holding this family firmly in his grace.

As if *sustaining* this trial with gratitude, hope, and contentment wasn't enough, the Fohners became literal endurance athletes of the highest caliber! They have *smiled* upon everyone their story has enabled them to meet, including the driver of the vehicle that struck Josh. They *share* God's glory through their suffering, trusting that he has chosen them for such a time as this.

Just like Jesus.

A SECOND CUP

 In her suffering, Kelly learned gratitude. In his suffering, Jesus learned obedience (Hebrews 5:8). What have you learned in your suffering?

 Read 1 Peter 1 and 3–5 in your Bible. Mark any passage about being chosen, called, elect, precious, and such with a diamond ring so that you won't forget that God chose you:

Dear heavenly Father, you alone have the power to sustain me through unimaginable suffering. I want to learn from each difficult experience and come out on the other side singing your praise. My hope is in you.
In Jesus's name, amen.

CHAPTER 3

HOW TO HANDLE AN UNHOLY MESS

1 Peter 3

I WAS MORE THAN A little lost driving on unfamiliar roads late at night when my exit sign finally emerged a few hundred yards ahead. I didn't see the other driver coming, but I felt the impact as her car slammed into mine when I changed lanes without looking. Time stood still as our cars spun in circles, glass flying and tires squealing. No one was injured, but both cars were demolished.

Even if you're a good driver, someday you might have a fender bender of your faith—or maybe your life is already totaled. These hard impacts can be the result of our own reckless behavior, or they can come out of the blue with no explanation or way of escape. Two questions immediately come to my mind during these freak accidents:

1. Why are you doing this to me?
2. What kind of woman do you want me to be?

I'll admit that the first question comes a lot faster than the second, which I only ask after hours (okay, days . . . or weeks) of angst, worry, fear, dread, panic, and so forth. My first reaction to suffering is a primal, self-protecting instinct with only one goal: make it stop. Whatever is hurting me or someone I love, whatever is confusing or difficult, whatever doesn't fit into my carefully constructed dreams and schemes: Make. It. Stop. My second reaction, which comes more quickly as my faith grows stronger (but still takes longer than it should), is to prepare my mind for action so that I can conduct myself in a way that honors God and brings him glory.

See, God is just as concerned with our reaction to circumstances as the circumstances themselves. What kind of people will we be when there's a bridge out ahead, when someone goes the wrong way down our one-way street, or another driver is barreling toward us at full speed? A crowd of onlookers is watching how you conduct yourself as your story skids out of control and waiting to see if you'll emerge from the wreckage.

Your conduct includes all the data the FBI could dig up on you. If someone fact-checked your life, what would they find in your bank statements, internet history, location tracking, texts, emails, deleted photos, and disappearing Snapchats? Your conduct reflects your integrity (or lack thereof). It's what you do when you think no one is looking. It includes good deeds (and the bad ones) and the actions you perform throughout your day. Conduct includes your words—every shout and whisper Alexa, Siri, or Google has overheard; every handwritten letter and hasty text; every correspondence and conversation; every word left unsaid—and those you wish you could take back. Your priorities, motives, thoughts, ideas, desires, decisions, and emotions are expressed through your conduct. Your conduct is all another person can ever know about you.

Your conduct is what you say and do that can be seen by others, and it's the theme in the third chapter of 1 Peter. Actually, Peter begins the conversation in chapter 2 and mentions it in every chapter. Whenever you read a passage about our conduct, behavior, or actions, draw a magnifying glass like this beside it to remind you that people are watching how you handle an unholy mess:

This chapter looks at household codes that governed 1 Peter's recipients. We'll see how these specific instructions still hold valuable applications for us today. Peter gives advice for our conduct in our cities, in our marriages, and at church. He also reveals a solid strategy you can use to navigate emotional traps, and we'll learn one simple question that will help you figure out how to respond in complex situations. My friend Jennifer's story provides proof that Peter knew what he was talking about, and she will share how a person can stay on track when life spins out.

 Scan this code or visit www.amylively.com/cup-of-hope /#chapter3 to access online resources and read the Scripture passages online.

Lesson 1

~ ❄ ~

Specific Instruction, General Application

Read 1 Peter 2:11–12

REMEMBER THAT TIME I TOOK a twenty-year detour on my journey with Jesus? I mentioned it in chapter 2 and promised we'd come back to it later, so here goes: From my midteens to midthirties, I disregarded the teaching of my godly parents and ignored their good example in my extreme efforts to fit in with the crowd and be liked, accepted, and popular. I justified myself with all the things I *wasn't* doing—I wasn't robbing banks! I wasn't a majorly bad person! I even went to church on Christmas, Easter, Mother's Day, Father's Day, and my parents' birthdays.

So many people shared that they took a similar side trip in their Christian walk when I wrote about this season in *How to Love Your Neighbor Without Being Weird*. If that's the story of someone you love, please never stop praying for their return. God never stops listening! If that's your story, you understand how much work it takes to ignore God. Hardening my heart took intention and practice. I made grocery lists in my head when the hymns made me cry. I didn't question God's role, but I resisted his rule; I didn't stop believing, but I stopped following. I could handle my own life.

This strategy was working fine for me until my marriage hit a crisis, and ironically it was my return to faith, not the lack thereof, that caused problems. I had come back to Jesus as a true fan . . . well, more like a fanatic. I went to church whenever they cracked the doors, could spout a Bible verse for any occasion, and used the sword of the Spirit like a lethal weapon. Debating doctrine was a form of entertainment to me. "The Bible says this . . ." or "I heard a sermon about that . . ." and "God is telling me to do whatever . . ." did not go over well with my husband, who didn't disagree with me in principle but didn't appreciate being used as my sparring partner.

We argued constantly, and divorce was mentioned for the first time. As our marriage skidded out of control, my husband finally said, "If God can't help us, no one can," and suggested we meet with the pastor of the church I'd been attending on my own. And do you know what my pastor said the first time he met my husband? He said, "Amy, you care more about expressing your opinion than the effect of your opinion." In other words, "Amy, shut up!" (or "be still" if you prefer a more genteel phrasing).

Back to the Bible I went, this time looking for ways to conduct myself instead of control other people. I did word studies on *opinion* and tried to listen instead of arguing. It took a while to undo the damage I had caused, but today my husband and I are closer than ever, by the grace of God. We survived this collision of our faith with real life, but it was a close call.

Peter was writing to baby believers like me, whose new beliefs, interests, and customs were shaking up their world—sometimes through no fault of their own and sometimes by their own failure. Peter gets bossy in this little book; he's got something to say to everyone. He gave *specific instruction* for first-century conduct for wives as well as husbands, citizens, slaves, church leaders, and youth. We will also discover *general application* for relationships and circumstances across all generations.

Household Codes

"Household codes" were an elephant in the room Peter had to address. These deeply ingrained rules dictated acceptable behavior in every sphere of first-century Greco-Roman life. Plato, Aristotle, Plutarch, and a bunch of other philosophers you haven't thought of since high school authored household codes to ensure social stability, economic prosperity, and family unity—and cooperation wasn't voluntary. Peter (and Paul, who also addressed household codes) didn't suggest that social norms be tossed out the window—this would have quickly gotten the early church squashed, because new religions were closely monitored to make sure they didn't upset the applecart of cultural norms.[1] Peter didn't endorse the rules, either, since many of them were in direct opposition to the gospel message of freedom, love, and humility. He began by clearly stating the purpose and intent of his newfangled New Testament code of conduct:

> Beloved, I urge you as sojourners and exiles to abstain from the passions of the flesh, which wage war against your soul. Keep your *conduct* among the Gentiles honorable, so that when they speak against you as evildoers, they may *see* your good deeds and glorify God on the day of visitation. (1 Peter 2:11–12)

Jews called anyone who was not a Jew a *Gentile,* and with these verses Peter is reminding us that these unbelieving neighbors are looking for any reason to discredit our testimonies. In the early church and still today, Christians find themselves exiled in a hostile land and under constant scrutiny. People are watching to see if we live up to our own claims. Does our faith make a difference in the way we live? Will we take the high road or trudge along in the mud? Will we ask for forgiveness when we fail or refuse to make peace?

Honorable conduct honors Christ. The Greek word for "honorable" is *kalos* (kal-*os*) and it means beautiful, handsome, excellent, praiseworthy, and precious. The reason we are called to conduct ourselves honorably is not just to stay out of trouble, make ourselves look good, or win points in heaven. When people see our good behavior during bad times, we point to a good, good Savior. When we are winsome, we will win some!

Next, we'll take a closer look at Peter's advice on how Christians should conduct themselves as citizens, at home, and even at church.

A SECOND CUP

 Share something you're zealous about besides your faith— for example, I love telling people about Aldi grocery stores, the AnyList app, and *Heartland*. Name a product, service, app, show, or store that you're a true fan of, that you think everyone in the world should know about.

 Envision one person you wish to influence through your conduct as you read 1 Corinthians 9:22. In what ways are they different from you? Consider their maturity, history, worldview, goals, interests, frustrations, and fears. How do these differences make this relationship difficult? Without compromising your morals or beliefs, how might you adjust your conduct to become more winsome to them?

 Peter was with Jesus as he preached the Sermon on the Mount, when he heard Jesus say, "Let your light shine before others, so that they may see your good works and give glory to your Father who is in heaven" (Matthew 5:16). What happened when Jesus did a good work in the following verses?

> Luke 5:26
> Luke 7:15–16
> Luke 13:13
> Luke 18:43

 How would you rate Peter on a scale of 1–10 for following Jesus's example in Acts 3:2–8?

 Read Galatians 1:24. What problems are you facing today that you might be able to shine light and give glory to God through?

 Read 1 Peter 3 in your Bible and draw a magnifying glass like this beside any passage about the desired conduct of a believer, to remind yourself that people are always watching how we act.

Dear heavenly Father, thank you for giving practical advice that's useful in every area of my life. Teach me how to apply your Word in everyday situations, so that you get all the glory. In Jesus's name, amen.

Lesson 2

⟋ ✦ ⟍

Conduct as Citizens and Slaves

Read 1 Peter 2:13–20

Do you think Peter had any idea about today's political scene when he wrote these words?

> Be subject for the Lord's sake to every human institution,
> whether it be to the emperor as supreme, or to governors as
> sent by him to punish those who do evil and to praise those
> who do good. (1 Peter 2:13–14)

The Roman Empire was forcefully expanding across three continents when Jesus appeared on the pages of history. Because Jesus's story is set during a time of civil unrest and aggression, each generation after has a model to follow in the worst of times under the harshest leaders. Modern US politics is mild compared with Jesus's world.

A few years before Peter wrote his letter, the emperor Claudius kicked all the Jews out of Rome (Acts 18:2). Ancient historians say this happened because the Jews and Christians were constantly rioting over a figure called "Chrestus"—probably Christ.[2] Despite Jewish opposition, the Christian church was growing explosively, and Claudius wasn't having any luck controlling it. By AD 41 he had limited their gatherings, demanded that they not travel to or welcome visitors from other cities, and forbade their sneaking into "gymnasiarchic games."[3] No, they weren't trying to slip into the gym without a membership: they were harassing the public performances where people were "being scourged, hung up, bound to the wheel, brutally mauled and haled for their death march through the middle of the orchestra."[4] By AD 49 Claudius had booted both the Christians and the Jews out of Rome completely, and this is how we find our "elect exiles" from 1 Peter 1:1 scattered across Pontus, Galatia, Cappadocia, Asia, and Bithynia.

Claudius was poisoned in AD 54, and his sixteen-year-old stepson, Nero, was declared emperor. Nero canceled all of Claudius's edicts, so the Christians and Jews were allowed to return to Rome. Nero liked sports and video games, like any teenager—but in his day this meant gladiators and coliseums. Nero loved going to the movies . . . I mean, the theater, and even made an appearance as an actor, which was considered exceptionally low-class. In the summer of AD 64, a terrible fire burned two-thirds of Rome. Nero blamed the Christians for the fire and retaliated with violence, which became his trademark. The historian Tacitus wrote:

> Mockery of every sort was added to their deaths. Covered with the skins of beasts, they were torn by dogs and perished, or were nailed to crosses, or were doomed to the flames and burnt, to serve as a nightly illumination, when daylight had expired. Nero offered his gardens for the spectacle, and was exhibiting a show in the circus . . .[5]

Complaints about today's political landscape in the United States pale in comparison to this ghastly regime or the persecution Christians in much of the world face today. When Peter talked about "fiery trial" (1 Peter 4:12) and described the enemy as "a roaring lion, seeking someone to devour" (5:8), his readers knew exactly what he was talking about. This cruel government was included in "*every* human institution" when Peter insisted on submission and obedience.

Conduct as Citizens

Peter doesn't tell us to be subject to our government only when our preferred party is in power. He doesn't tell us to honor rulers only if we voted for them. He doesn't even tell us to obey laws only if they are to our advantage. Not only when we feel like it . . . when it's easy . . . when it's convenient . . . when we agree . . . no, no, nope. There's only one qualifier to this command: do it for Jesus.

It's for the Lord's sake that we obey. Go back and circle this phrase in 1 Peter 2:13. Does our Christian faith extend to driving the speed limit, paying our taxes, and respecting law enforcement officers? You betcha. Does that mean that I like speed traps or think marriage penalty taxes are fair or that police officers can use excessive force? Absolutely not. When we see injustice, we are duty bound to act upon it in a way that honors Christ. Run for office, write your government officials, protest peacefully, learn about your local issues, educate your circle of influence—then intervene, intercede, and inspire others. I'm so thankful for people God has called to ministry in government!

How would Jesus vote? I have no idea! But we have seen him submit to every human institution—even the one that would scourge and crucify him. We know he paid taxes (Matthew 17:24–27), and I do believe Jesus would drive the speed limit—just one of the many reasons he is a much better witness than I.

> For this is the will of God, that by doing good you should put to silence the ignorance of foolish people. Live as people who are free, not using your freedom as a cover-up for evil, but

living as servants of God. Honor everyone. Love the brother-hood. Fear God. Honor the emperor. (1 Peter 2:15–17)

It's not enough that we *not* do bad things; we must actively do good—and not just to our governing authorities. Peter tells us we must conduct ourselves honorably toward *everyone*. Like literally every single person. Our sanctimonious or sarcastic Facebook posts won't change people's minds. Our rants and petitions won't change the world, but our good deeds will win hearts.

Our ultimate authority is God alone, and Peter tells us to conduct ourselves as "servants of God." Various translations say we should live as bondservants or slaves. The Greek word Peter uses is *doulos* (*doo*-los), the term for a servant who does the will of someone else. A *doulos* of God is a metaphor for someone who is fully submitted to Christ, willing to do his will no matter the cost. Believers are to function within the larger community, honoring everyone and submitting to the government, by living as servants of God, a greater authority than any human institution.

Conduct as Slaves

In verse 18, Peter transitions to addressing specific roles in society, beginning with household servants. Don't let the translation "servants" bring to mind a maid or butler in a well-pressed uniform: they were slaves. Well-to-do Roman families had household slaves, and many of our early church brothers and sisters counted themselves among the quarter of the population that were servants.[6] To them, Peter wrote:

Servants, be subject to your masters with all respect, not only to the good and gentle but also to the unjust. For this is a gracious thing, when, mindful of God, one endures sorrows while suffering unjustly. For what credit is it if, when you sin and are beaten for it, you endure? But if when you do good and

suffer for it you endure, this is a gracious thing in the sight of
God. (1 Peter 2:18–20)

It's painful to imagine the suffering of the 46 million people who
are legally enslaved in over 165 countries today[7]—not to mention
those who are trafficked *illegally* in small towns and big cities across
the United States and other parts of the free world. Slavery in this
first-century society was often as cruel, demeaning, and abusive as it is
today. Slaves and their families were considered personal property of
their owners. Sometimes the poorest families, in desperation, would
sell their children to survive.[8]

Contrary to cultural household codes that emphasized the roles of
people who held power and control, Peter's letter is remarkable in that
he addresses servants at all. By doing so he values the most vulnerable
people in God's kingdom. And yet Peter asked slaves to show respectful submission during undeserved suffering. Free and justified before
God, they remained bound to be submissive to unjust masters.

Any general application for this specific instruction is going to require God's grace, Jesus's humility, and the Holy Spirit's power. Yet we
must ask: If this is Peter's charge for ancient slaves, what might he say
to the modern Christian?

Peter gave slaves a higher calling than the command of their masters, and he gives the same to us. God is whom we ultimately obey and
trust. We may be free to live where we want and work when we please,
but we are never free from our calling as Christians. God is delighted
when we respond to meanness with kindness, when we show respect
even as we are disrespected, or when we give our best effort as others
show their worst side. Our good conduct when we are treated badly
points to God's grace.

When Abraham Lincoln was just a young man working as a store
clerk in the early 1830s, abolitionists, many of whom were Christians,
began the work that would eventually end slavery in America. The

American Anti-Slavery Society held meetings where freed slaves could share their stories. They proposed legislation and sent petitions to Congress, printed journals, and mailed antislavery propaganda leaflets by the thousands.[9] Their messages were destroyed and their printing presses burned—but they pressed on. They prevailed even though it took over thirty years of preaching before President Lincoln helped end slavery for good. Their objective was to oppose moral corruption with moral purity, destroy error with the potency of truth, and overthrow prejudice by the power of love.[10] We should take cues from this strategy today as we hold abusers accountable and boldly confront injustice.

Peter's encouragement is that followers of God should lead by faithful example in order to influence even the harshest of naysayers. Mindful of the Father, the only begotten Son endured sorrows while suffering unjustly (1 Peter 2:19). Jesus became gentle and lowly so that weary workers could find rest for their souls (Matthew 11:29). He is the overseer who notices the ignored, cares for the cast off, protects the exposed, and elevates the unseen.

A SECOND CUP

We read in 1 Peter 2:13 that it's "for the Lord's sake" that we obey. How is this concept stated in Ephesians 5:21–22? How does submission to others "for the Lord's sake" alter your perspective?

How has faith become intermingled with politics? Are you able to identify biblical teaching for each of your dearly held political beliefs? How might our country be affected if we filtered current events through our faith first instead of solely through a political affiliation?

What injustice do you see in the world that makes your heart grieve? How might God use you in this situation to reveal his glory?

 How does your faith impact how you handle difficult situations? Give an example of a time when your conduct was different from others because of your beliefs.

Dear heavenly Father, I want to be your servant as I serve others. Please guide me in your ways, so that I stand out as wonderfully weird in public settings—more loving, more caring, more kind than anyone expects or deserves. In Jesus's name, amen.

Lesson 3

⁓ ❧ ⁓

Conduct at Home and Church

Read 1 Peter 3:1–7 and 1 Peter 5:1–5

I WOULD NEVER ACCUSE THE women in Peter's audience of being as annoying about their new beliefs as I was, but they had problems of their own. First-century wives (and servants, too) were expected to worship the gods of their husband; the philosopher Plutarch even went so far in his household codes as to restrict a wife's friendships:

> A wife ought not to make friends of her own, but to enjoy her husband's friends in common with him. The gods are the first and most important friends. Wherefore it is becoming for a wife to worship and to know only the gods that her husband believes in and to shut the front door tight upon all queer rituals and outlandish superstitions. [11]

Perhaps you understand the dilemma of a wife who is madly in love with Jesus and at the same time in love with a man who isn't. There's nothing ancient about this scene. It's one that has played out in every generation. As I learned in my marriage, it's hard on relationships when an eager new believer's interests and activities change. But it's difficult for us to imagine how much changing one's allegiances and defying cultural expectations could bring harsh consequences to a first-century home. A husband who couldn't control his wife was publicly scorned as weak and ineffective and could be denied certain honors and offices.[12] If the wife wasn't worshipping the household gods, she could be blamed for any misfortune or calamity the gods were thought to bring on the family. A wife had little recourse if her husband retaliated.

Conduct at Home

When Jesus is the model for our household codes, Plutarch and his pals don't stand a chance! Peter's letter again goes against prevailing cultural norms to respectfully address the most vulnerable members of society:

> Likewise, wives, be subject to your own husbands, so that even if some do not obey the word, they may be won without a word by the conduct of their wives, when they see your respectful and pure conduct. (1 Peter 3:1–2)

Peter preaches that husbands who do not believe *the Word* will be won over *without words* when they observe their wives' pure and reverent conduct, so I tried this on my own husband. I thought if he saw me praying and going to church, he'd want to pray and go to church, too. I read my Bible every day and followed all the rules—and helpfully pointed out when he didn't. I made church my number-one priority at the expense of caring for my family.

The classic Amplified translation brings out a deeper truth: husbands who don't believe *the Word* will be won over *without words* when they see how their wives treat *them* . . . not how their wives treat *God*.

> When they observe the pure and modest way in which you conduct yourselves, together with your reverence [*for your*

husband; you are to feel for him all that reverence includes: to respect, defer to, revere him—to honor, esteem, appreciate, prize, and, in the human sense, to adore him, that is, to admire, praise, be devoted to, deeply love, and enjoy your husband]. (1 Peter 3:2 AMPC)

When I stopped trying to convert my husband to my way of thinking and focused on connecting in ways that were meaningful to him, we were able to walk toward God together.

Peter's specific advice is true in marriage, and it's a general principle we can apply to other relationships as well. Only when people see how we behave toward them will they care about us or our beliefs. You've probably heard the saying "People don't care how much you know until they know how much you care." This is both a relief and a burden to me: it's a good thing I am not personally responsible for arguing, debating, lecturing, nagging, or coercing anyone into the kingdom of heaven, but at the same time, it's hard for me to listen well and keep my opinions to myself. I've learned that loving silence can preach louder than spoken words.

Next, Peter meddles in a woman's wardrobe:

> Do not let your adorning be external—the braiding of hair and the putting on of gold jewelry, or the clothing you wear—but let your adorning be the hidden person of the heart with the imperishable beauty of a gentle and quiet spirit, which in God's sight is very precious. (1 Peter 3:3–4)

What gives Peter the right to comment about a woman's clothing and appearance? Do these comments seem old-fashioned or misogynistic to you? What's so bad about looking good?

We could confine this statement to the first century by saying it was a command that was only applicable in their outdated culture, but really, not much has changed in women's fashion trends. In their world, only wealthy aristocrats could afford fine clothes and jewelry and had servants to braid their hair. Some styles of clothing were indicators of an immoral lifestyle or pagan worship. Today our choice of clothing still signals our economic position and worldly priorities. And while there's nothing sinful about looking one's best, Peter affirms that a woman is worth so much more than what can be seen and admired on the outside. The Greek word Peter used for "adornment" is *kosmos*, which is the root of the word *cosmetics*. If your whole world revolves around cosmetic beauty on the outside, it's easy to ignore the hidden person of the heart. God sees your heart—he really *sees* you—and it's precious to him when your spirit is gentle and peaceful, "calm and self-controlled, not overanxious, but serene and spiritually mature" (AMP) because you hope fully in him.

Peter isn't a chauvinist; in fact, he extends this specific instruction to all of us:

> Clothe yourselves, all of you, with humility toward one another, for "God opposes the proud but gives grace to the humble." (1 Peter 5:5)

Peter holds all of us, not only women, to the same dress code as Jesus:

> There was nothing beautiful or majestic about his appearance, nothing to attract us to him. (Isaiah 53:2 NLT)

This verse tells us that Jesus wasn't considered attractive or stunningly handsome. Furthermore, as Jesus made his way to the cross, a purple robe was laid across his bloody shoulders to make fun of his claim to royalty. A crown not of gold but of thorns was pressed into his hair. Yet Jesus clothed himself with honor and humility even as he was despised and rejected, oppressed and afflicted. What they meant for mockery, he turned to glory—and this is now our privilege and calling. Could there be any higher standard of beauty than Jesus?

Peter now turns his pen to the husband. (Don't worry, we're not skipping over the verses about wives submitting to their husbands and calling him lord in 1 Peter 3:5–6; this will be covered in "A Second Cup.")

> Likewise, husbands, live with your wives in an understanding way, showing honor to the woman as the weaker vessel, since they are heirs with you of the grace of life, so that your prayers may not be hindered. (1 Peter 3:7)

Jesus calls men to a loftier standard than the world sets. Do you think Peter's wife suggested he add this part before mailing his letter? It's hard work for husbands to understand their wives, yet Peter tells men it's their responsibility to make this effort. The Amplified Bible says men are to live with their wives "with great gentleness and tact, and with an intelligent regard for the marriage relationship." By choosing the Greek word *gnosis* (*no*-sis), which means knowledge, intelligence, and understanding, Peter implies that this is the science of relationships, an advanced education in Women 101. Men who fail this class will find their prayers faltering, as will any Christ follower who has war in their heart while they pray for peace.

Jesus did more to elevate women than any other man in history, and this command to honor women as co-heirs is revolutionary. You saw that, right? Or did you get stuck on the "weaker vessel" part? This is easily true in a physical context since men have more muscle mass, denser bones, larger hearts and lungs, faster recovery from wounds, less tendency to depression and anxiety disorders, and on average six extra inches of height than women.[13] In a cultural context, men reading Peter's letter had higher social standing, more legal rights, and greater access to education than women had. Peter had no tolerance for a husband who used physical strength or social power to abuse or misuse his wife, nor should the church today.

Peter's expectation was that households committed to Christ would be held to a higher calling. Jesus leveled the imbalance of power between men and women forevermore by showing that we should treat those who have set their hope fully on God's grace as kingdom co-laborers and equal partners in the gospel.

Conduct at Church

Members of the Christian church must also model Christlike conduct. Peter addresses leaders first in chapter 5:

> So I exhort the elders among you . . . : shepherd the flock of God that is among you, exercising oversight, not under compulsion, but willingly, as God would have you; not for shameful gain, but eagerly; not domineering over those in your charge, but being examples to the flock. (1 Peter 5:1–3)

Spiritual leadership in the Christian church is based on calling and qualification. Sadly, shameful gain and domineering authority aren't limited to any generation or denomination, so this warning stands for all churches of all time. This passage says as much about the congregation as it does the elders: we desperately need godly instruction and oversight because we, like sheep, are prone to wander.

Peter follows his advice to the elders with advice to the youngers:

> Likewise, you who are younger, be subject to the elders. (1 Peter 5:5)

If you don't hold the recognized position of elder in your church, this verse applies to you regardless of the number of candles on your birthday cake. To be subject to our church leaders means to conduct ourselves with respect, to heed their counsel and instruction, and to obey their biblical requests.

I didn't envy church leaders as they navigated the pandemic. I'm sure I was cause for their groaning with my grumbling when our elders requested that we not meet in small groups, even when it was technically allowed by our county health department. I had to make a conscious, difficult decision to conduct myself with submission and obedience. These general principles can be extended to positions of leadership in the church, workplace, home, or community: Lead with integrity and enthusiasm for the glory of God and not personal gain. Follow respectfully, carefully, and kindly.

A SECOND CUP

Read 1 Peter 3:3–6 and Genesis 18:1–16 about Sarah, a "holy woman who hoped in God." How did the Lord react to Sarah's laughter (Genesis 18:9–15)? Read the Lord's response to Sarah in Genesis 18:15 aloud in a scolding tone, then again in a lighthearted or laughing tone, and explain which you think the Lord used. How do you think the Lord responds to your doubts and questions?

Peter says in verse 6 that women are as esteemed as Sarah if they "do not fear anything that is frightening." Do you think Peter implies that submission can be frightening? Is submission frightening to you? What was Sarah afraid of in Genesis 18:15? Was she being asked to submit to God or to man? What is scary about submitting to someone else? To God?

Visualize in your mind the scene from Genesis 18, with yourself as Sarah. Where was she standing, what was she doing? How was she included or excluded from the conversation? What emotions might she have been feeling? Thousands of years later, this is the scene Peter points to as an example of a godly wife and follower of God. Whether you are married or not, what hope does this give you?

 Peter quotes Psalm 34:12–16 in 1 Peter 3:10–12. If your role in life has left you feeling fearful, ashamed, ignored, or overwhelmed, meditate on Psalm 34. What promises are found in each of the following verses: Psalm 34:4, 6, 7, 9, 15, 17, 18, 19, 22?

Dear heavenly Father, I see that my relationships can only thrive when I put you in the center. May my eyes see only Jesus as I decide how to conduct myself at home and at church. Help me to trust your power over my problems and follow your ways instead of my wishes.
In Jesus's name, amen.

Lesson 4

~ ❖ ~

Feel, Real, Deal

Read 1 Peter 1:15–16 and 1 Peter 3:3–16

SWIMMING LAPS IS MONOTONOUS FOR me unless I'm mad about something. One sunny morning when I was particularly annoyed, I fitted my goggles over my cap and poured my heart out in prayer while I swam. I let loose an unfiltered litany of complaints, accusations, and justifications about a conflict I'd had with a friend (good thing I was underwater where no one could hear me!).

Working out helped me work on a tangle of emotions, and I had an epiphany after a few hundred yards: I want to live by feelings, but I expect others to live by facts.

- I *feel* overwhelmed; don't they *know* how busy I am?
- I *feel* unappreciated; don't they *know* how much I do for them?
- I *feel* lonely; don't they *know* they should include me?
- I *feel* misunderstood; don't they *know* that's not what I meant?

How easily I let feelings and emotions rule my thoughts and actions, all the while expecting others to respond according to facts and truth!

What if I switched this around? What if I asked the Holy Spirit to remind me what's *real* before being controlled by what I *feel*? Here are some relevant truths I discovered:

- They love me.
- They handled that poorly.
- They are also under pressure.
- They have my best interest at heart.
- I was rude.
- I didn't communicate well.

My emotions weren't the problem. They were neither "good" nor "bad"—they simply *were*—and I needed to feel all the feels before I could move on. Some of my feelings were justified and needed to be shared; others were selfish and needed to be shelved. I walked (or swam) around all sides of the situation and shone the light of truth upon it until I was able to see my own contribution to the conflict and have compassion on theirs. I saw God's hand working through a hard situation and remembered his promises and commands. Scripture came to mind that I studied when I returned to dry land, and I decided how to deal with my friend in a way that would be honoring to myself, to her, and to God. Once I acknowledged how the situation made me *feel*, I was able to see what was *real*—and then I prepared my mind for action to *deal* with the situation. Feel, real, deal.

Having emotions isn't my problem. My problem is when my emotions have *me*. Our thoughts should control our emotions, not the other way around. If our thoughts are based on truth and facts, our emotions become a powerful motivator for positive conduct. If our emotions are in control of our thoughts that drive our actions, we tend to wallow in self-pity and self-righteousness. And chocolate. But maybe that's just me.

You've heard we should ask, "What would Jesus do?" but I'd also like to know, "What would Jesus think?" and "What would Jesus feel?"

Peter looked to the suffering of Christ as our perfect and primary example. Our relationship with Jesus should affect how we relate to everyone else.

What's the Holy Thing to Do?

As Christians, we have rules that supersede our roles, and the bar for our behavior is set very high:

> But as he who called you is holy, you also be holy in all your conduct, since it is written, "You shall be holy, for I am holy."
> (1 Peter 1:15–16)

When I want clear and specific instructions about how to handle life's suffering—a voice from heaven would be nice!—God sends his Spirit to softly whisper, "What's the holy thing to do?" Peter has more to say to all of us:

> Finally, all of you, have unity of mind, sympathy, brotherly love, a tender heart, and a humble mind. Do not repay evil for evil or reviling for reviling, but on the contrary, bless, for to this you were called, that you may obtain a blessing. For "Whoever desires to love life and see good days, let him keep his tongue from evil and his lips from speaking deceit; let him turn away from evil and do good; let him seek peace and pursue it. For the eyes of the Lord are on the righteous, and his ears are open to their prayer. But the face of the Lord is against those who do evil." (1 Peter 3:8–12)

God stands with the crowd of bystanders watching how you conduct yourself. They're watching to see what will happen when the immovable object of cultural expectations meets the unstoppable force of a sympathetic, loving, tender, and humble Christian. In the sight of

God, it's a gracious thing when you do good and endure suffering because of it (1 Peter 2:20). To him, a gentle and quiet spirit is a precious thing to behold (1 Peter 3:4). But when God spies someone perpetually plotting evil, he averts his eyes and can't fulfill their prayers. Don't let that someone be you!

We've lived enough days to know that life isn't fair. But God does care. Jesus empowers the oppressed. God does not tolerate our prejudices and partialities. He comforts the persecuted. He elevates the lowest position to the seat of highest esteem—then asks us to yield once more and humbly submit to one another. Could there be a timelier word in today's uncertain times? Peter leaves us with this final strategy:

> In your hearts honor Christ the Lord as holy, always being prepared to make a defense to anyone who asks you for a reason for the hope that is in you; yet do it with gentleness and respect, having a good conscience, so that, when you are slandered, those who revile your good behavior in Christ may be put to shame. (1 Peter 3:15–16)

When life hands you an unholy mess, God will help you figure out, "What's the holy thing to do?" Be prepared to respond when (not *if*) you are slandered because of your faith in God, when your loved ones don't love Jesus, or when people make a mockery of your magnificent Savior. There ought to be something wonderfully odd about the way you handle your life that makes people consider, "Hey, how'd she do that?" How did you respond with grace when they know you wanted to growl? What held you together when life looked hopeless? How did you keep breathing when your world crumbled around you? With the evidence of your conduct on display for all to see, they will ask you to give a reasonable explanation. You will finally be able to release all the words you've been holding in as you gently and respectfully share why you hope fully in God's grace.

A SECOND CUP

Peter hadn't yet perfected the Feel, Real, Deal strategy when he faced the following situations. Read the passages below and answer the Feel, Real, Deal questions to explain how Peter handled himself. When you're under pressure like Peter was, what's your first response?

Matthew 26:69–75
Mark 9:2–10
Luke 9:28–36
John 21:20–22

Feel	Real	Deal
What do you think Peter was feeling in this moment?	What was the larger truth about Peter's situation?	How did Peter deal with the circumstances?

Think of a challenging situation you're facing, and prepare your mind for action by developing a spiritual strategy:

Feel	Real	Deal
What do you feel about what's happening? Pour out your emotions.	What is real about this situation? Write down facts, truth, and evidence.	Make a plan for how to deal with the situation in a godly way.

In your own words, define *gentleness* as it applies in 1 Peter 3:15. Define *respect*. Give yourself a grade on gentleness and respect in the last interaction you had

when you were asked to defend your hope. If you haven't discussed your faith with anyone recently, why do you think that might be?

Dear heavenly Father, when my emotions overwhelm me, please remind me to think through all sides of a situation. Help me craft a godly response instead of a self-centered reaction. In Jesus's name, amen.

Lesson 5

— ❊ —

Jennifer's Story

Read 1 Peter 3:1–2

Swimming laps didn't become part of my life until I was in my midforties and decided to try a triathlon. My friend Jennifer made sure I was able to finish the first segment. She met me at the YMCA in the wee hours of the morning so we could finish our practice before our kids woke up for school. Being able to watch her underwater when I had never swum a lap in my life helped me learn how to maximize each stroke. And not drown.

Jennifer and I met when we moved to the same elementary school in the middle of the same school year (that's also when we both met our future husbands for the first time). We became close friends in college because our boyfriends were friends, and one year and one week after I was in Jennifer's wedding, she was the very pregnant matron of honor in mine.

Jennifer and her husband flourished in our small town. Their picture-perfect life was lined up across the mantel as wedding pictures were quickly followed by those of a beautiful baby girl, then a bouncing boy, then another son—and don't forget the golden retriever. They had the cutest house; he had the best job; they had the most adorable children. Jennifer thrived as a stay-at-home mom caring for their active kids and her successful and busy husband.

We've always had the kind of friendship that can withstand long times apart then pick up comfortably right where we left off. During one of those reunions after too many months apart, Jennifer and I sat on her sectional as I shared my excitement about my newfound faith— something that had never been part of our friendship before. I told her how God was blessing so many areas of my life, and I was attending church and soaking up his Word.

As our coffee cooled, I asked her, "So where do you stand with your faith?"

"I'm on the fence about God," Jennifer shrugged. Having been raised in a mainline Protestant church, Jennifer had a fundamental knowledge about God and craved a deeper relationship with him but didn't feel she could bring it home and live it out. She visited my church a couple of times, but it didn't go over well as it was quite different from the liturgy and prayers she was accustomed to. "I was used to going to church and just returning to my normal life without much thought," she said.

Despite the fairy-tale appearances, Jennifer began to sense something wasn't quite right. Her fire for life and joyful enthusiasm for people had been on a slow downward slope for several years, and she struggled to find her usual confidence. She couldn't put her finger on why she had become negative and distrusting of people, looking for the bad instead of the good. She didn't like what she was becoming, but she couldn't define it, either. She began to question the rumblings beneath the still surface that made her toss and turn at night, although her husband assured her there was nothing to worry about. She thought about getting a job, going back to school, or doing something outside the home to improve her self-esteem.

She was elbow-deep in dish suds when her TEOTWAWKI moment explained it all.

Her husband had left on a business trip that morning, so she was confused to see him standing in their kitchen. "We need to talk," he said. "You're right. I'm having an affair."

Jennifer didn't even wipe her soapy hands as she grabbed her purse and left. As she sped away from home, she realized her spiral from "I love life!" to "I don't even like people" was most likely caused by her husband's infidelity and betrayal. She had grown concerned over the years about a particular relationship that didn't seem appropriate at times. Whenever she questioned her husband, he told her it was nothing more than a casual friendship in their large, long-standing social group. Once the truth was revealed, scattered puzzle pieces came together and formed a disturbing picture.

She found me in the coffee-scented hallway of my church and told me what had happened. As we wept, she wondered what to do next. Would her children be okay? Would her life ever be the same? What about the plans for their future, let alone her hopes and dreams?

Our early mornings together began in earnest. It's a good thing we love coffee, because she would come to my house at five or six o'clock in the morning to pray and get her daily bread, a single verse to sustain her through the day. Sometimes it didn't last until the afternoon, and she'd show up again before dinner.

Her husband stayed in their home as they worked on their marriage. Jennifer and I worked on *her*—the only thing she could actually control. "God knocked me off the fence!" she's able to laugh now, grateful she landed on the right side. We focused on Peter's specific advice to wives:

> Likewise wives, be subject to your own husbands, so that even if some do not obey the word, they may be won without a word by the conduct of their wives, when they see your respectful and pure conduct. (1 Peter 3:1–2)

We made a plan of conduct so that Jennifer could hold her head high no matter what happened. Since this was long before texting, I emailed Bible verses for a jolt of encouragement. We meditated on powerful psalms that gave her rock-solid strength to handle this unholy mess (you'll find them in "A Second Cup"). Church and her spiritual family became essential to Jennifer. "I poured myself into the Word, and God was so faithful to bring people into my life to help me. Our pastor's messages had perfect timing. I saw more and more of God's faithfulness as he reached me through other people and his Word."

Jennifer clung to a teddy bear I gave her with a Bible verse on a heart around its neck:

Bear with each other and forgive one another if any of you has a grievance against someone. Forgive as the Lord forgave you. (Colossians 3:13 NIV)

"From the beginning, that became my motto. I was going to bear with all of this we were going through together. For some reason, I didn't have a problem forgiving him because I knew that had to be the foundation of reconciliation. I took that bear to heart!"

We talked a lot about how Jennifer should respond to her husband and children, and those nosy neighbors digging for gossip on their public drama. "I had probably told you something inappropriate that I wanted to say to them," Jennifer recalls, "and I'll never forget how you put down your coffee cup, leaned back in your chair, and said, 'You know, if it feels really good, you probably shouldn't say it.'"

Jennifer wore a beaded bracelet to remind herself to catch her tongue when she was tempted to respond sharply. "Boy, did that save me! I knew my tongue was a fire, and I did not want to cause any more turmoil than there already was. I didn't want to have any regrets about something I said that moved us backward instead of forward. I learned not to speak in the heat of my anger, to wait until I was calm to say what needed to be said in a gracious way."

Forgiveness, holding her tongue, memorizing Scripture, and deep times of prayer were central to Jennifer's survival strategy. She immersed herself in the church and a circle of godly girlfriends who met in the early mornings to study God's Word.

"There were definitely times when I could not see Jesus or feel his presence," she reminisces. "Those were probably the times I tried to take things into my own hands, trying to fix something or play detective. One of those times, I asked a question I wasn't prepared to hear the answer to. I had a very dark moment and ended up running away from home—it was childish, but I just had to get away." She only made it a few miles when she found herself sitting in a coffee shop, visibly upset. "A gentleman came up to my table, knelt beside me, and asked if he could pray for me. When I felt all alone, God sent this man to lift me up with a powerful prayer." She returned home to celebrate one of her children's birthdays, as if her world wasn't crumbling around her.

Back at that kitchen sink one day, struggling to figure out what to do, she raised her hands in literal surrender. "I can't do this! I want to do it your way, but I don't even know what that is!" she prayed. "When I finally gave up my plan of trying to do things my way and asked God to take the lead, I felt an inexplicable warm peace washing over me." She knew then she would survive.

"See me, praise thee!" was one of the mantras Jennifer lived by, praying that her gracious and forgiving conduct would glorify God. She knew God is not arbitrary in creating his high standards for our conduct; there is reason and purpose behind specific instructions like this:

> Be careful to live properly among your unbelieving neighbors.
> Then even if they accuse you of doing wrong, they will see

your honorable behavior, and they will give honor to God when he judges the world. (1 Peter 2:12 NLT)

Each morning she prayed, "What's the holy thing to do?" She continually asked, "How should I react to this trial? Where has God placed my way of escape from an unholy response? Who can help me find the righteous way? Who is watching to see if I fail? Are there specific instructions for this scenario or general biblical principles I can apply? Can I release my hopeful, happy ending into God's hands? Does my conduct show that my hope is set fully on the grace to be given when Christ is revealed? How can I respond in a way that glorifies God? What is the pure, righteous, sacred, and holy thing to do?"

"I was so hopeful that my husband would choose me. I hoped I would be the chosen one," Jennifer remembers. "I was hopeful that our marriage would be restored, and there would be reconciliation."

But after two years, her husband moved out. Two years after that, their divorce became final. Those years were formative and powerful in Jennifer's home. With two kids still in high school, she shared devotions with her sons during breakfast and hosted a new Young Life club, which still thrives today.

Looking back at our journals from that time, Jennifer and I find ourselves in awe at how many prayers God answered. She had prayed that God would help her notice her children's needs and that they would not become bitter or angry. (They didn't.) She prayed for financial details to wrap up so she could make decisions about her future. (They did.) She even prayed for her ex-husband to be comforted, knowing he must be missing the children. (He was.) Amid all these prayer requests, we had one prayer above all others: her ex-husband's salvation. Her youngest son was especially concerned about his dad, and they often prayed for him together. "It was one thing when you would pray for him," she says, remembering our many coffees on the patio, "but I knew I had turned a corner when I was able to pray for him with our son."

Eight years after Jennifer's TEOTWAWKI moment at the kitchen sink, her ex-husband, Johnathan, attended a funeral at the church where I was on staff. And he kept coming back. We were preaching a sermon series on neighboring, and we had noticed that Johnathan was actively involved in planning neighborhood activities where he lived. We asked him to share with the congregation how he connected with the people who lived near him, and I promised him that's as far as the questioning would go . . . but apparently I forgot to mention this to the pastor who was interviewing him.

"Anything else you want to share, John?" the pastor asked after their easy conversation about being a good neighbor. "Tell us about what's been going on in your life."

Johnathan's whole demeanor changed as he told the story of coming to the church for his friend's funeral. "No sooner than I sat down, the sound system popped—bam! I seriously wondered if God was sending me a message."

"So you've not lived a perfect life?" the pastor kidded. "You don't have to go into that. But tell us why you decided to make God a part of your life."

"My ex-wife, Jennifer, and our kids are very into their church and quite spiritual," Johnathan said. "Quite frankly, I saw them growing and developing. I was impressed and moved by it, and I want to be part of that."

And just like that, the apostle Peter's words to wives came to life.

Our prayers were not answered in the way we hoped. They certainly didn't happen when we thought. It took years before we watched the promise of 1 Peter come true. Our prayers for restoration and reconciliation of Jennifer's marriage were not answered, but God did redeem her ex-husband's heart.

Several years after the divorce, Jennifer reconnected with an old high school flame who is committed to the Lord; they married in 2015 and now enjoy a loving, Christ-centered home, walking faithfully with God together. Today, each of Jennifer's children and their families walk closely with God and are raising her grandchildren in his ways.

"I've had other earth-shattering TEOTWAWKI moments since then," says Jennifer. "Because I have been able to see God work in a dark time in my life—work through me, work for me, and be on my side, putting people in front of me, and the timing of certain things happening—I know he is in control." Her parents both passed away within months of one another while she was providing hospice care for her mother-in-law, during a difficult pregnancy for her daughter and the premature birth of her first grandchild, as her youngest son was graduating from college. "It was a challenge to hope fully that God was leading me through each situation, but I trust him with all my heart."

Be holy.

Be like Jennifer.

Be like Jesus.

A SECOND CUP

 What relationship do you feel is under scrutiny as bystanders watch to see how you'll react? Who's watching your conduct in your community? At work? At home? At church?

 From an email I sent to Jennifer before one of our early morning prayer times, here are several psalms to meditate on when you're handling an unholy mess:

Psalm 40—My Help and My Deliverer

Psalm 86—Great Is Your Steadfast Love

Psalm 91—My Refuge and My Fortress
Psalm 116—I Love the Lord

 Visit www.amylively.com/psalms to download a pretty printable of Scripture to sustain you, or scan this code:

 Think of someone whose conduct has caused you to give glory to God. What did they do that called attention to our Father rather than themselves?

 As a reminder to mind your conduct, read 1 Peter 1–2 and 4–5 and draw a magnifying glass by references to conduct, behavior, actions, or other people who are watching us.

Dear heavenly Father, thank you for giving me the tools I need to deal with all life's trials. Please open my eyes to the people watching and listening to me when I am unaware. May you be glorified in my every word and deed! In Jesus's name, amen.

CHAPTER 4

BEFORE AND AFTER

1 Peter 4

My husband and I have enjoyed renovating several houses. Our first was the home he grew up in, and we made it our own with ivy wallpaper and white cabinets in the kitchen. One of our homes was a seventies discotheque that we practically demolished—it was so ugly, I could barely see through my tears to sign the purchase contract. We made over a mid-century cabin in the Rocky Mountains into a stunning modern farmhouse, and we turned a shabby trailer into a chic vintage getaway. I love to compare before-and-after pictures of dingy, dated rooms to the bright new spaces that have been fixed up exactly the way we envisioned when we moved in.

It was fun renovating those outdated houses . . . but it's not so fun to redo my own soul. No matter how much I try to paint over my old sins and insecurities, they still bleed through. In the Before pictures of our lives, bad habits are like a cracked foundation, and unhealed wounds leave stains. I want to fast-forward to the magical reveal of my picture-perfect life.

Unfortunately, there's no time-lapse video or entertaining thirty-minute program for the laborious process of our suffering being transformed into worship, anxiety being turned to trust, and fear being made over to faith. Following Jesus is a lifelong process of soul renovation that Peter knows more about than most, as we'll see in his story—and apply to ours. The tool Peter gives us to tear down the wall that divides our will from God's isn't in our hands; it's in our minds.

The contrast between our old self and our new self is a theme in 1 Peter. Whenever you read a verse about this contrast, draw a simple circle with a line through the center to divide the Before and After, the then and now, the old made new, like this:

We'll spot this theme of contrast throughout Peter's letter but most noticeably in 1 Peter 4. Peter encourages us to stop doing whatever we want, whenever we want, however we want to do it (living in the flesh for our human passions) and start doing what God wants in the way he wants (living for the will of God). We'll see how our view can be clouded by our own opinions and desires and learn three ways that Jesus brings us into perfect agreement with his plans. Finally, you'll meet a new friend, Sarah, who will vulnerably share how God moves us from tragedy to triumph during a painful, glorious transformation.

 Scan this code or visit www.amylively.com/cup-of-hope /#chapter4 to access online resources and read the Scripture passages online.

Lesson 1

⟶ ❖ ⟵

Soul Renovation

Read 1 Peter 4:1–6

I TAKE BEFORE-AND-AFTER PHOTOS OF the renovation projects my husband and I tackle together, but there are some memories that can't be captured digitally (or on film, but that would be dating myself). Like the intensity in my husband's eyes as he painted the trim in a corner of our first home, mindful of the tiny details. Or wrestling with wallpaper that didn't come pre-pasted, and the residue of wallpaper glue that's caked on the heavy folding table we still use as a desk. Or rolling on four coats of paint in the nursery while I was eight months pregnant because I bought cheap materials. We've laughed, cried, discussed, debated, fought, and high-fived over nine homes in five states in thirty-plus years and counting, enduring numerous rounds of demolition and reconstruction for the joy of creating a home for our family.

There's a big difference between buying a fixer-upper and deciding to tackle the difficult, costly, and inconvenient work you know it will involve and, say, having your house destroyed by a tornado. Some suffering roars at us like a cyclone, unexpected and uncontrolled, mangling everything in its path. But there's a kind of suffering we willingly commit to endure when we give God permission to wreck us in every way, which we'll see in 1 Peter 4.

Suffering Is a Way of Thinking

As you'll discover in Peter's story, his Before pictures were a disaster. He made promises he couldn't keep. He put his foot in his mouth when he spoke without thinking. He could be argumentative and power hungry. Yet Jesus looked into the eyes of this mess of a man, chose him as one of his closest friends, and called him as his first disciple. If God can renovate Peter, he can do the same for us. The reason we hold Peter in such high regard today is because God empowered him to follow Jesus with all his heart, receive the Holy Spirit, and surrender himself to the Father's will—even if that meant suffering. With his eyes affixed on Jesus, Peter learned that suffering requires a certain way of *thinking*:

> Since therefore Christ suffered in the flesh, arm yourselves with *the same way of thinking*, for whoever has suffered in the flesh has ceased from sin, so as to live for the rest of the time in the flesh no longer for human passions but for the will of God. (1 Peter 4:1–2)

Peter's life and his letter show that suffering is more than what happens *to* you; it's what happens *in* you when you give God his way in your life. We do more than begrudgingly submit to this kind of suffering. We willingly step into it. We think long and hard about what it will cost us to obey the will of God. It may cost us humiliation with our friends because we no longer participate in the sin-centered activities we used to enjoy together. It may cost us embarrassment as we refuse to engage in neighborhood gossip or risk as we speak up for the oppressed. We may have to lay aside our rights and consider others as more important than ourselves—ouch! Like Peter and his wife, some Christians must decide if they're willing to risk their very lives by proclaiming their faith. Christians carefully evaluate the cost and make an informed decision to pay the high price of following Jesus. This kind of suffering is a voluntary self-sacrifice that costs us something dear.

Since we can't banish suffering, we must let God transform us into better sufferers. Transformed suffering means trusting, loving, sharing, praying, serving, worshipping, praising, and glorifying God during our hardest moments—even choosing to allow these moments to happen. Suffering happens *in* you and *with* God, as you are wrapped in his grace, sustained by his power, purified by his Spirit, and cleansed by his Son as you cry, "Here I am to do your will. I give all I am for your glory!"

The Apprenticeship

When we start working on our soul-improvement projects, we work side by side with the Holy Spirit. We co-labor with the Holy Spirit as his apprentice to complete transformations like these:

> In this [salvation] you rejoice, though now for a little while, if necessary, you have been grieved by various trials, so that the tested genuineness of your faith—more precious than gold that perishes though it is tested by fire—may be found to result in praise and glory and honor at the revelation of Jesus Christ. (1 Peter 1:6–7)

During our suffering, it takes the Holy Spirit's help to move from sorrow and sadness to singing songs of praise. If we keep our eyes on our salvation instead of our circumstances, grievous trials can become times of rejoicing, and tests of our faith will result in praise and glory and honor to Christ. Let's visualize this contrast:

	Before	After
1 Peter 1:6	Grieved by trials	Rejoicing in salvation
1 Peter 1:7	Test of faith	Result of praise

In the last chapter of 1 Peter, we see another amazing transformation that requires our cooperation:

> Humble yourselves, therefore, under the mighty hand of God so that at the proper time he may exalt you, casting all your anxieties on him, because he cares for you. (1 Peter 5:6–7)

Before, we fought against the mighty hand of God, worming our way out from under his authority and squiggling under his power—but wait, I'm sharing my own experience again. Perhaps you could say this, too. Perhaps you, like me, used to envision God's heavy hand pinning you down in a tight, controlling grip. The Holy Spirit helps me see God's open hand reaching toward me, ready to receive and relieve my worries and cares, lifting me up to safety. See the contrast in our soul before and after this renovation:

	Before	After
1 Peter 5:6	Humbled low	Exalted high
1 Peter 5:7	Carrying my anxieties	Casting them on God

We are transformed when we permit the Holy Spirit to deconstruct the habits, hurts, and hang-ups that would hinder us from a full, free life. God's great care for us is our safety net.

Call the Pros

Some home projects are so ambitious and complex that we have to call a professional contractor, like building an addition or rewiring the electricity. In our hearts, the transformation from sinner to saint is a renovation project so huge, God himself has to do it for us. Like a toddler with a voltage tester trying to rewire a house, we're utterly incapable of accomplishing the scope of this project on our own. Let's look at a few examples Peter provides in his letter:

> As obedient children, do not be conformed to the passions of your former ignorance, but as he who called you is holy, you also be holy in all your conduct, since it is written, "You shall be holy, for I am holy." (1 Peter 1:14–16)

Just be holy? Me? Yeah, I'm going to need an instruction manual (preferably with words, not just cartoons like IKEA) and some YouTube videos to complete this project. Peter gives a negative command in this passage—"do not be conformed"—instead of providing concrete action steps. And he calls us unintelligent and lacking knowledge (or at least we used to be). Before we knew that God's clock is set for eternity, before we understood we are chosen, and before we realized the importance of our conduct, we were just a wee bit ignorant. Maybe we had simply never been shown a better way.

Back then, in our Before pictures, we lived for our passions. Our own desires and outcomes determined our plans. We lusted after beauty, or possessions, or success, or money—whatever filled our thoughts, we sought. Like Eve eating the forbidden fruit, we indulged anything that looked good to the eyes and seemed right at the time, no matter the consequences. Peter likes the word *passions* so much that he used it three more times in 1 Peter:

1. In 2:11, he tells us to abstain from passions of the natural-born flesh which wage an all-out war against our born-again soul.
2. In 4:2, he tells us to live the rest of the time—our After pictures—no longer for human passions but for the will of God.

3. And in 4:3, he said the time is past for doing "evil things that godless people enjoy" (NLT), a life of unrestrained passions and shameful immorality.

But now? After we've met Jesus? Now we're striving for holiness instead of settling for happiness. As obedient children, we pause to ask our Father what to do, what to think, how to be. "What are you doing today, Lord, and how have you invited me to be part of it? Who have you placed around me to love today? Where are we going next, Daddy?" This after picture is an eager, trusting, compliant child holding her Father's hand, looking into his eyes, seeking his smile and guidance. We can only become holy with God's help, and he's here for it. Here's a diagram as God erases the contrast between our sin and his grace, our fallenness and his faithfulness, our grime and his glory:

	Before	After
1 Peter 1:14	Ignorance	Obedience
1 Peter 1:15–16	Passionate	Pure
	Want to be happy	Want to be holy

The Master Carpenter

Jesus is the Master Carpenter who teaches us how to construct a life that pleases our Father. Peter wants us to follow Jesus's example so closely that he uses the same words to describe what Jesus did and what we should do:

Jesus	Us
When he was reviled, he did not revile in return; when he suffered, he did not threaten,	Do not repay evil for evil or reviling for reviling… 1 Peter 3:9

Jesus	Us
but continued entrusting himself to him who judges justly. 1 Peter 2:23	…let those who suffer according to God's will entrust their souls to a faithful Creator… 1 Peter 4:19

Peter offers more comparisons of what our lives should look like now that we're disciples of Jesus. He tells us to stop nibbling on malice, deceit, hypocrisy, envy, and slander, and instead reach for pure spiritual food (1 Peter 2:1–2). We won't take part in excessive partying anymore (1 Peter 4:3). Even though confused friends will spread gossip because we no longer go along with them (1 Peter 4:4), we only offer a blessing in return (1 Peter 3:9). Several times Peter warns that even if we've done nothing bad, we may suffer badly (1 Peter 2:19–20; 3:17; 4:14–15). The contrast Peter calls for will look like this:

	Before	After
1 Peter 2:1–2	Unhealthy snacks	Pure spiritual milk
1 Peter 2:19	Beaten as sinners	Beaten as saints
1 Peter 3:9	They curse	We bless
1 Peter 4:3	Partying	Piety
1 Peter 4:4	Scandalous life	Slanderous lies

Jesus hands us the blueprint to build our own cross. For his sake and with his help, we crucify our Before selves to experience the After life.

A SECOND CUP

What's your favorite decorating show, magazine, or website? How would you describe your style? On a scale

of 1–5, how much do you enjoy home improvement projects?

1	2	3	4	5
I'd rather hit my thumb with a hammer.	I have a handyman on speed dial.	I can hang pictures.	I have tools and know how to use them.	I should have my own reno show!

 Read the following before-and-after passages and write in your journal the differences between our old selves and new selves:

> **Colossians 3:5–17**
> **Ephesians 4:17–5:14**

 Which room in your heart needs an extreme makeover? Where is God calling you to trust his wrecking ball and let him renovate your old self into a new creation? Possibilities include your marriage, parenting, finances, habits, mental health, or any part of your life that needs to be rebuilt.

 Read 1 Peter 4 in your Bible and draw a divided circle beside any verse about the contrast between our old self and new self, like this:

*Heavenly Father, please wreck me in the best possible way. Transform my impure desires so that all I want is your perfect design. Rebuild me in your image.
In Jesus's name, amen.*

Lesson 2

~ ❖ ~

Heaven Forbid

Read Matthew 16:13–17:8

LIKE MOST OF PETER'S LIFE lessons, learning how to think about suffering happened the hard way for him. It began right after Peter's bold declaration that Jesus is the Christ, the Son of the living God. Jesus affirmed Peter's confession and replied:

> "Blessed are you, Simon son of Jonah. . . . On this rock I will build my church. . . . I will give you the keys of the kingdom of heaven; whatever you bind on earth will be bound in heaven, and whatever you loose on earth will be loosed in heaven." (Matthew 16:17–19 NIV)

In biblical times, *binding* and *loosing* were terms the disciples would have heard often from their rabbis, who used their authority to judge what was permitted or not permitted. They had so many rules and regulations that Jesus accused them of shutting the door to the kingdom of heaven in people's faces (Matthew 23:13).

Jesus didn't hand Peter a big ring of jangly keys that unlock the

Pearly Gates (although this passage is why Peter is often depicted standing at heaven's gate, deciding who gets in). The keys to the kingdom of heaven signify the gospel message that unlocks eternal life with Christ for those who believe. Jesus gave Peter the authority to throw open the doors of heaven and invite the whole world to come in!

Oh Peter, Did You Really?

Having told the disciples who he was and why he'd come, Jesus proceeded to let them in on his agenda for the days ahead—and it didn't sound good. In no uncertain terms, Jesus explained that he would "suffer many things from the elders and chief priests and scribes, and be killed, and on the third day be raised" (Matthew 16:21). I imagine the scene as Peter listened to this terrible warning. His eyebrows might've shot up, and he might've physically recoiled at the gruesome picture Jesus painted. This didn't fit with the plan! But then Peter remembered: he had just been handed the keys to the kingdom of heaven! He believed he had authority to declare that this terrible outcome was not permitted. Peter sidled up to Jesus, took him by the elbow, and whispered, "Hey, can I talk to you in private for a minute?"

> Peter took him aside and began to reprimand him for saying such things. "Heaven forbid, Lord," he said. "This will never happen to you!" (Matthew 16:22 NLT)

Oh Peter . . . you didn't really reprimand Jesus, did you? Yes, he did! Peter thought enough of himself and his newfound authority that he had the nerve to correct Jesus. He talked to the Son of God like he was a child, and the one who was supposed to be following tried to be the leader. Isaiah asked the rhetorical question:

> Who is able to advise the Spirit of the LORD? Who knows enough to give him advice or teach him?" (Isaiah 40:13 NLT)

Peter thinks he is able; he believes he knows enough to offer Jesus advice and teach him a thing or two. A beautiful new hymn repeats that same question from Isaiah, and whenever we sing "Behold Our God" at church, I look around to see if anyone else in the sanctuary is raising their hand to respond, "Umm . . . me? I do! All the time, in fact." Apparently, Amy and Peter are the only ones who can admit our attempts to boss God around.

Jesus then turned to Peter and gave him one of the sharpest rebukes in Bible history, saying,

> "Get behind me, Satan! You are a hindrance to me. For you are not setting your mind on the things of God, but on the things of man." (Matthew 16:23)

In just a few verses Peter went from "Blessed are you, Simon!" to "Get behind me, Satan!" Right after Jesus called Peter the rock upon which he would build his church, he called Peter a rock of stumbling, a hindrance, a trap. That's not quite the contrast we're aiming for, is it? But I get it. I'm right there with Peter, heaven forbidding all my worst fears:

> *Heaven forbid sickness or disease. I want health.*
> *Heaven forbid conflict. I want peace.*
> *Heaven forbid painful consequences. I want everything to go smoothly.*
> *Heaven forbid change and upheaval. I want things to stay the same.*
> *Heaven forbid I lack anything. I want it now.*
> *Heaven forbid all pain, grief, difficulty, sorrow, and sadness. I want an easy life.*

I can just imagine you nodding with me right now. If we, Amy and Peter, got our way, we would've "heaven forbidded" everyone we love out of any agony, ever, including Christ off the cross. What Peter didn't understand at the time (and what I struggle with today) is the splendor on the other side of suffering. Without crucifixion, there is no resurrection, no salvation, no eternal life. When I have in mind "the things of Amy" instead of the things of God, I miss his greater glory and highest purpose. Without dying to myself, I cannot live for Christ.

Jesus called this kind of misguided thinking an act of Satan. It wasn't the first time Jesus dealt with the devil, and it wouldn't be the last. Satan wasn't done with Peter yet.

Flip the Script

Jesus used Peter's outburst to show the kind of contrast he's looking for in our lives:

> "If anyone would come after me, let him deny himself and take up his cross and follow me. For whoever would save his life will lose it, but whoever loses his life for my sake will find it." (Matthew 16:24–25)

The key that unlocks the mystery of suffering is the same key that unlocks the kingdom of heaven: it's the gospel of Jesus Christ. Jesus shows us an upside-down and inside-out way of living . . . and of dying. Can you imagine how horrific it sounded to Peter and the other disciples to hear Jesus say, "take up your cross"? They regularly witnessed criminals being crucified in Jerusalem, and it was a fate you wouldn't wish on your worst enemy. Some two thousand years after the crucifixion, we have a complete understanding of the cross. We already know the ending, but what Peter heard was only the beginning of Jesus's teaching about what true suffering looks like.

Before, we would do anything we could to save our life, preserve our rights, and protect our best interests. We avoided pain, sacrifice, and hardship at all costs. But after? After we meet Jesus, we deny ourselves by setting aside our selfish interests. After, we are willing to endure whatever he asks, even suffering to the point of literal, physical death.

Jesus flipped the script and turned winning into losing and dying into living. The daily pain of dying to ourselves and the sacrifices we make for others bring the most gain. This is all that counts in Christ's kingdom.

This is how Jesus lived, and this is how he died. He always had in mind the things of God more than the things of Peter or Amy. Our holy Savior stepped down into our sewage, tossed his crown, and took up his cross. He gave up his life to save ours in the most horrifying, humiliating way so that we could share his glory and receive his grace.

Sticks and Stones

Mountain highs can descend into valley lows at whiplash speed, as Peter experienced when he went from blessed confessor to cursed distractor in the blink of an eye. Just a few days later, this dizzying drop would happen again when Jesus took Peter and two other disciples on a mountain hike. This scene, known as the Transfiguration, is found in Matthew 17:1–8, but let's make a note of two details found in the parallel passage in Luke that will be important to us later: Jesus took the disciples to the mountain to pray, but Peter fell asleep (Luke 9:28–35).

While Jesus prayed, he was transfigured into a dazzling white vision the disciples barely recognized. The prophets Moses and Elijah appeared with Jesus, and heaven touched earth on that mountaintop for just a few moments as the keepers of the old covenant talked about how it would be made new.

Jolted from sweet dreams, Peter jumbled his words and said, "Lord, this is awesome! Let's build three tents, one for each of you!" Jesus's transfiguration may have taken place around the time of the Jewish Feast of Tabernacles, a yearly celebration of the harvest that also recalled their wilderness wandering. During the festival, each family constructed a temporary tent shelter from olive branches, palm fronds, twigs, and leaves, and lived in it for a week.

As soon as the words left Peter's mouth, a cloud descended on them and they heard the thunderous voice of God say, "This is my Son, my

Chosen One; listen to him!" (verse 35). God's admonition echoed Peter's confession a few days earlier: Jesus is the Christ, the Anointed and Chosen One, the Son of the living God. Instead of bossing Jesus around as he was wont to do, Peter was warned to listen.

If Peter had been praying instead of sleeping and listening instead of talking, he may have caught on that Jesus was not interested in a temporary shelter made of sticks but an enduring church made of stones—living stones, as a matter of fact—starting with Peter himself. Peter was getting ahead of God's big plans with his own small ideas.

When we summit the mountain and catch a glimpse of the glorious After, we're eager to leave Before behind. God gives mountaintop inspiration in small doses, only as much as we can handle at one time, because he knows our tendency to rush the renovation he is doing in our souls. Mountaintop experiences are crucial moments as we draw close to God, letting him fill our hearts with knowledge, revelation, and fellowship—but we can't stay there. When we enter the inevitable valley where life feels hard and suffering gets real, we draw on what we learned and experienced on the peak. If we're not careful to listen to Jesus by spending time in prayer, we may plunge ahead in the wrong direction like Peter did, missing the plans Jesus has made for us right where we are.

A SECOND CUP ————————————————————

Peter argued with the Lord four times. Draw a line to connect the passage with the issue Peter argued about:

Matthew 16:21–23	Partiality, prejudice
Matthew 26:30–35	Spiritual cleansing
John 13:1–11	Suffering
Acts 10:9–35	Falling away, failure

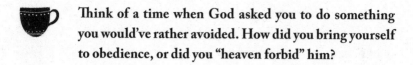

Think of a time when God asked you to do something you would've rather avoided. How did you bring yourself to obedience, or did you "heaven forbid" him?

Read about Jesus's upside-down life in Philippians 2:5–8. Draw a sketch of where Jesus started and where he ended. What was the outcome for Jesus as described in Philippians 2:9–11? Compare this passage with 1 Peter 5:10. What is God's promise to us if we trust him with our suffering?

How has the Lord surprised you with something bigger, better, and more wonderful than you ever imagined, as in Ephesians 3:14–21?

➤

Dear heavenly Father, suffering is hard. I have dreams of a good and simple life, but that seems out of reach sometimes. You ultimately have good in mind for me, and I need your help to trust you completely. In Jesus's name, amen.

Lesson 3

Out of Darkness

Read Luke 22:24–34, John 13:1–11, Mark 14:32–42,
and Luke 22:54–62

IF YOU'VE EVER STRUGGLED TO keep your family celebrations civil, you know exactly what Jesus dealt with. In the middle of the most important Jewish holiday of the year, Peter and the disciples got into an argument at the dinner table about who was the greatest. They acted like little children who roll up their shirtsleeves, compare their tiny, flexed biceps, and throw down an arm-wrestling contest right over the centerpiece. Ever kind and wise (and more patient than any of us could be), Jesus paused the Passover meal to break up the disciples' argument for an important lesson in contrast:

> And he said to them, "The kings of the Gentiles exercise lordship over them, and those in authority over them are called benefactors. But not so with you. Rather, let the greatest among you become as the youngest, and the leader as one who serves. For who is the greater, one who reclines at table or one

who serves? Is it not the one who reclines at table? But I am among you as the one who serves." (Luke 22:25–27)

The kingdom culture is so distinct from the world that it's difficult to comprehend. Outside of Jesus's circle, authorities rule with a tight fist and powerful title. "But not so with you," Jesus teaches. Christ's followers don't lord over others, they serve under them. The only title they're interested in is *servant*. The greatest guest at dinner sits at the children's table, and the waitstaff earns the highest reward. This is what kingdom contrast looks like:

	Before	After
Luke 22:25–27	Lord over	Serve under
	Greatest	Least
	Leader	Servant
	Guest	Waiter

It's just like Peter (okay, me, too) to be caught up in the middle of a power struggle, but things would get worse for Peter before they would get better.

The Sifting

While they were still gathered around the table, Jesus turned to Peter and uttered this chilling warning:

"Simon, Simon, behold, Satan demanded to have you, that he might sift you like wheat, but I have prayed for you that your faith may not fail. And when you have turned again, strengthen your brothers." (Luke 22:31–32)

Satan only has so many tricks up his sleeve, and sifting is one of his favorites. I've seen it happen countless times in my ministry. Women regularly contact me about starting a Neighborhood Café Bible study in their home after seeing resources on my website or hearing me speak. They're always so eager at first, full of enthusiasm to share coffee, conversation, and Christ with their neighbors in their home. I listen to their ideas and offer suggestions and always pray with them, but then I must warn them: their initial excitement will turn to angst as the inevitable sifting begins. Satan will shake up their confidence to convince them they're unqualified. He'll rattle their family as arguments overheat. He will wallop them in their pocketbook and put a strain on their health so that they become overwhelmed. He will stir strife in the neighborhood. Our work is too important for the devil not to care!

The same thing happens after a rich conference, impactful retreat, summer camp revival, or even a great sermon. Whenever Satan senses someone on a spiritual high, he tries to bring them low. Sometimes your suffering is because you're up to something good! He's a rotten little devil who will stop at nothing to distract us from our kingdom calling. Satan hates your transformation from your old passions to your new holy self. It enrages him. He will use every opportunity to remind you that you are failing. You are lacking. You are stuck in your ignorance. Your shame makes you stink.

He tried to do it to Jesus. Right after Jesus was baptized, a humble act of obedience that God honored with a public display of his pleasure (Matthew 3:13–17), Jesus was led by the Spirit into the wilderness to be tempted (Matthew 4:1–11).

Three times, Satan offered Jesus a shortcut to avoid suffering.

Three times, Jesus stood firm.

Jesus gave Satan the same scolding he would later give Peter: "Be gone, Satan!"

If Peter had been listening instead of talking, he may have thanked Jesus for his prayers and asked for help to withstand the sifting. Instead, Peter cockily replied:

"Lord, I am ready to go with you both to prison and to death." Jesus said, "I tell you, Peter, the rooster will not crow this day, until you deny three times that you know me." (Luke 22:33–34)

Peter miscalculated Satan's schemes and his own strength, a strategy that would hurt him greatly.

The Crowing

After supper, Jesus modeled a striking example of what he'd just taught by washing the filthy feet of his followers (a scene at the Last Supper table told only in the Gospel of John). Jesus washed Peter's feet, overcoming his loud objections with soft servitude. Jesus washed Judas's feet, knowing the devil would soon lead Judas's steps to the soldiers who would arrest Jesus.

Jesus took Peter and the other disciples to the Mount of Olives just a short distance away to pray. Peter, James, and John accompanied Jesus a little farther into a garden called Gethsemane, where Jesus asked them to stay awake with him and pray, but they could barely keep their eyes open. Jesus, clearly upset, jolted Peter from his sleep as he'd had to do before at the Transfiguration:

And he came and found them sleeping, and he said to Peter, "Simon, are you asleep? Could you not watch one hour? Watch and pray that you may not enter into temptation. The spirit indeed is willing, but the flesh is weak." (Mark 14:37–38)

Three times, Jesus asked Peter to watch and pray with him.

Three times, Peter fell asleep.

Peter's willing spirit could not overcome his weak flesh, and his good intentions couldn't overcome his bad habits. Jesus was transfigured as he prayed, but Peter remained unchanged as he slept. The sifting began its slow rumble as Peter slumbered.

As Jesus knew would happen, Judas found him in the garden and betrayed him with a kiss. Jesus was arrested in Gethsemane and taken to the home of Caiaphas the high priest, while Peter lagged at a distance. The disciple so quick with fiery responses now warmed himself by a charcoal fire in Caiaphas's courtyard, where he was questioned about his relationship with the man from Nazareth. Within hours, Peter's brash readiness to go with Jesus both to prison and to death was replaced with refusal to even acknowledge his name:

> A servant girl, seeing him as he sat in the light and looking closely at him, said, "This man also was with him." But he denied it, saying, "Woman, I do not know him." (Luke 22:56–57)

I wouldn't be surprised to hear this denial from a prideful atheist or a pondering agnostic—but from a professing believer, it's difficult to understand.

Peter's denial was a lie . . . or was he telling the truth? In that moment, we might wonder, did he really know Jesus? He could still feel Jesus's fingers washing dirt from between his toes, a menial task Peter didn't want to allow. The emotional breakdown Peter witnessed in Gethsemane was unlike any outburst he'd ever seen, and he might have even been embarrassed by it. Peter left everything to follow this charismatic preacher who was now letting himself be led away in chains. Did Peter think Jesus was giving up just when they were gaining ground? Did he question how their movement would end Roman rule if Jesus just rolled over? The man Peter had seen transfigured into a bright white vision of hope was nowhere to be found. This was not what he signed up for. No, Peter did not know this man.

I wonder, do you? Have you been bitterly disappointed when

following Jesus doesn't look like you imagined? Do you think your goals seem further away than ever and time is running out? Do you wonder why Jesus didn't listen to your advice when you suggested an easier way? Peter's denial is not so difficult to understand when I see how I have denied Christ in my own life.

Three times, Peter was asked if he knew Jesus.

Three times, he denied it.

And the rooster crowed.

The courtyard where Jesus's trial and Peter's denial might have taken place is now beneath a church in Jerusalem, which is called the Church of Saint Peter in Gallicantu. *Gallicantu* is Latin for "cock's crow." I once thought roosters were like a morning alarm clock that gave a cheery cock-a-doodle-doo at dawn. My neighbors have a rooster, and let me tell you, that bird crows all day long, and often at night, with an ear-splitting screech. A rooster crowing in Jerusalem, even at night, wasn't such a strange thing. Jesus chose a traditional wake-up call to remind Peter that he should have been awake and praying instead of sleeping, and I bet that rooster's crow sounded like a victory wail straight from hell.

A golden rooster is perched atop the dome of the Church of Saint Peter in Gallicantu, which is built over the remains of first-century caves and cisterns. Visitors today can peer into a cellar where Jesus may have been taken after the rooster crowed and his sham trial commenced. As he spent a night in captivity, one can imagine his own cries:

> I am counted among those who go down to the pit; I am a man who has no strength. . . . You have put me in the depths of the pit, in the regions dark and deep. . . . You have caused my companions to shun me; you have made me a horror to them. I am shut in so that I cannot escape. . . . You have caused my beloved and my friend to shun me; my companions have become darkness. (Psalm 88:4, 6, 8, 18)

If your Bible has headings before the chapters, you may see this Psalm called "A Prayer for Help in Despondency." Pastor and author Dr. Paul Tripp calls it "A Psalm That Has No Hope."[1] Beloved friend, Jesus knows your suffering when someone has sinned against you. He is intimately familiar with suffocating darkness when you are rejected, scorned, denied, betrayed, and accused.

Peter also knows your pain. He failed to live up to his own expectations and everyone else's. He must have believed he had messed up beyond redemption, that he was beyond all hope.

What began as a rumble as Peter slept became a bone-rattling, earth-quaking tremor in his walking nightmare. Jesus had called him out of the darkness, and he had missed the step into his marvelous light.

A SECOND CUP

When have you experienced this statement: "Sometimes suffering is because you're up to something good!"? Think of a time you had a mountaintop spiritual high immediately followed by a valley low. Why do you think Satan wanted to sift you? Were you on the verge of taking a big step of faith? How did God prepare and protect you? Read Job 1 for a similar story.

Which do you think was more painful for Jesus—the betrayal of Judas or the denial of Peter? When have you been hurt deeply by someone close to you? In your life before Christ, how would you have been tempted to respond? What is the contrast in your response after following Christ?

Who do you know who is being sifted (perhaps even yourself)? Read Luke 22:32. When Jesus saw this coming for Peter, he didn't pray that Peter would avoid the trial—he prayed that Peter would stand strong during the trial and use it to strengthen others. How should this encourage and direct our prayers?

 Write out Genesis 50:20 and Romans 8:28. What hope do these verses give us when we're being sifted and shaken? What does God promise the outcome will be? What hope does this give us during our trials?

Dear heavenly Father, please uphold me when my faith is being shaken. I can only be restored by your grace. Even when I don't understand, please give me faith in your plan. In Jesus's name, amen.

Into His Marvelous Light

Read 1 Peter 2:21–25, John 21:1–19, Acts 2:1–4, and 1 Peter 5:10

THIRTY OR SO YEARS AFTER his horrendous night, Peter picked up his writing stylus to write the short letter we hold in our hands today. The night of his betrayal was still vivid in his mind. He would never forget how the soldiers taunted Jesus and spit on him. Peter remembered how he had watched from a safe distance as Jesus was falsely accused, publicly scorned, and viciously beaten. He remembered the voice he'd heard on the mountaintop—"This is my Son, my Chosen One; listen to him!"—but how Jesus spoke no words in his own defense. Peter knew Jesus could have called on countless angels in an instant but didn't. Peter heard the hammer strike the nails into Jesus's hands and feet and saw the sword pierce his side. When Jesus heaved his last breath, Peter ran and hid.

Peter's own sins were etched in his mind when he penned these words for us:

· He himself bore our sins in his body on the tree, that we might die to sin and live to righteousness. By his wounds you have been healed. (1 Peter 2:24)

It was Peter's own sin he saw on that tree, sin so great and grievous that it made Jesus bleed. Peter had abandoned the Christ, denied his best friend, and caved at simple questions from a servant girl. What gave Peter the right to tell us to "die to sin and live to righteousness"—the ultimate before-and-after contrast? If we can answer these questions for Peter, we can apply the solutions for ourselves. Three critical incidents helped Peter understand how Jesus's wounds had healed his sin, enabling Peter to finally step out of the darkness into the marvelous light.

Incident 1: The Face

It's hard to imagine that Peter could ever forget the first time Jesus looked at him. He was fishing with his brother, Andrew, who had been trying to convince him that the Messiah they'd been praying for their entire lives had truly arrived. Andrew took him to meet the man that a strange prophet in the wilderness had been raving about. Peter would never forget Jesus's face:

> Jesus *looked* at him and said, "You are Simon the son of John. You shall be called Cephas" (which means Peter). (John 1:42)

The intensity in Jesus's eyes made Peter believe Jesus could see all the way through to his soul—and Peter knew the depth of sin and darkness Jesus would find there. Peter may be known as the first to confess that Jesus was the Messiah, but he was also the first to confess his sins as he responded, "Depart from me, for I am a sinful man, O Lord" (Luke 5:8).

Peter would see the intense look of love in Jesus's face again when Jesus was approached by a rich young man trying to check off all the religious boxes and earn his way to heaven. Knowing the man would walk away sad because he couldn't pay the ultimate price, Jesus looked at him with love:

Jesus, *looking* at him, loved him. (Mark 10:21)

Peter had seen Jesus turn his face and look with love upon sinners and scoffers, diseased lepers and desperate souls, demon-possessed people and prideful hypocrites, those who would hate him and the ones who would embrace him.

In Caiaphas's courtyard, Peter saw the look another time (all three of these passages use the same Greek word for *look*):

> But Peter said, "Man, I do not know what you are talking about." And immediately, while he was still speaking, the rooster crowed. And the Lord turned and *looked* at Peter. And Peter remembered the saying of the Lord, how he had said to him, "Before the rooster crows today, you will deny me three times." And he went out and wept bitterly. (Luke 22:60–62)

And the Lord turned and looked at Peter. I find this to be one of the most heart-wrenching sentences in the entire Bible, and I think the hurt in both of their faces must've been unimaginable. We need to see ourselves in this scene. "And the Lord turned and looked at Amy." Could we ever sin again if we saw Jesus turn to look at us in the middle of our offense?

There is nothing you could ever do that would cause Jesus to turn his face away; there is no crime you could commit for which he has not already received your punishment in his body on the tree. From the cross he turns his face toward you and looks at you with lovingkindness, not scorn. When you weep bitterly with Peter over your failures, you're met with the unflinching, ever-loving gaze of Jesus.

Incident 2: The Feast

The second incident happened a few weeks after Peter's betrayal. Jesus had risen from the dead just like he said he would, and he had appeared at separate times to different disciples. On this morning, Peter and the others were fishing in the Sea of Galilee when they recognized Jesus on the shore. Our always-impetuous Peter jumped into the water with his clothes on and swam to shore to greet his Savior. Jesus prepared breakfast by the sea with fish and bread cooked over a charcoal fire. After breakfast, Jesus asked Peter if he loved him. Then he asked again. And again.

Three times, Jesus asked if Peter loved him.

Three times, Peter affirmed that he did:

> Peter was grieved because he said to him the third time, "Do you love me?" and he said to him, "Lord, you know everything; you know that I love you." Jesus said to him, "Feed my sheep." (John 21:17)

Three times. Around a charcoal fire. Do you see what Jesus did there? Peter denied Jesus before his enemies, but he was restored before his friends. Jesus undid what Peter had done, offering threefold forgiveness and reconciliation. No matter how many times you do wrong, Jesus gives you as many chances to make it right.

Incident 3: The Flame

The final incident happened exactly fifty days after Jesus rose from the dead, and ten days after he ascended into heaven. Up to the moment he was taken from them, the disciples were still asking when Jesus would restore power to the nation of Israel. They were in Jerusalem, waiting for a mysterious gift Jesus had promised to send them. They were together in one place when the gift arrived, and as usual, God did more than they expected:

> And suddenly there came from heaven a sound like a mighty rushing wind, and it filled the entire house where they were

sitting. And divided tongues as of fire appeared to them and rested on each one of them. And they were all filled with the Holy Spirit and began to speak in other tongues as the Spirit gave them utterance. (Acts 2:2–4)

When bystanders heard the ruckus and accused them of being drunk at 9:00 in the morning, Peter set them straight. In fact, Peter stood and lifted his voice and loudly declared exactly who Jesus was and why he came! The denier became the proclaimer that day. Peter preached and preached, and the church grew and grew—and neither ever stopped.

Peter described the Holy Spirit in three unique ways:

- The Spirit of Christ (1 Peter 1:11)
- The Holy Spirit sent from heaven (1 Peter 1:12)
- The Spirit of glory and of God (1 Peter 4:14)

The Holy Spirit wasn't impersonal or incomprehensible to Peter; he was an intimate friend. Peter heard the rushing wind and felt the air pressure in the room change when the Spirit arrived. He felt his skin tingling and his hair blowing. He saw flames burning over the heads of his closest friends and knew there was one on him as well. His heart raced as the flame entered his soul and burned the darkness away. He felt fellowship with Christ return to him. The long-awaited gift Jesus promised had finally arrived from heaven! The same Spirit that rested on Peter comes to dwell with you, too:

If you are insulted for the name of Christ, you are blessed, because the Spirit of glory and of God rests upon you. (1 Peter 4:14)

How to Cross the Line

Cathedrals are built in Peter's honor, cities around the world are named for him, and schools and banks in Rome close each year on June 29 to remember their patron saint with regattas, parades, and fireworks. Are we talking about the same guy? How did he cross the line from sinner to saint? How did this miserable failure become world-famous, let alone qualified to write the letter we're studying today? He gave us the answer himself:

> For you were straying like sheep, but have now returned to the Shepherd and Overseer of your souls. (1 Peter 2:25)

Peter strayed, but Peter stayed. He returned to Jesus and never wavered again. Peter didn't return to the Shepherd and Overseer of his soul because Peter was especially good, or qualified, or gifted. He didn't become a saint because he suddenly stopped sinning. He crossed the line from darkness to light because Jesus crossed the line from death to life. Peter crossed the line because Jesus prayed for him:

> "Simon, Simon, behold, Satan demanded to have you, that he might sift you like wheat, but I have prayed for you that your faith may not fail. And when you have turned again, strengthen your brothers." (Luke 22:31–32)

Jesus warned Peter that Satan was out to sift him like wheat. Peter uses a much more graphic image in the final contrast he leaves us to consider:

> Be sober-minded; be watchful. Your adversary the devil prowls around like a roaring lion, seeking someone to devour. Resist him, firm in your faith. (1 Peter 5:8–9)

After his own bout with Satan, Peter recognized him as a sneaky opponent and powerful enemy. Then he shares the strategy he probably wished he'd had in place. Be sober-minded so you can hope (1:13), so you can pray (4:7), so you'll survive (5:8). Be watchful and careful, paying close attention to the traps he's laid for you. Resist the devil, ready to fight for your life. Be firm in your faith, immovable and strong. Be steadfast now so you can stand fast later.

	Before	After
1 Peter 5:8–9	Drunkenly inattentive	Soberly standing firm

I hate to be the bearer of bad news, but remember when Jesus said Satan demands to have *you*, that he might sift *you* like wheat? That means you, as in you personally. The Greek construction of this sentence uses the plural form of *you*, which includes Peter and all the disciples. Still today, disciples who follow Jesus will be sifted like wheat and stalked like prey—but you already know that. You've felt it, and you might even be living through it right now. And the rest of the passage where Jesus says he is praying for *you*, that *your* faith will not fail, that *you* will return and strengthen *your* brethren—that's the singular word for *you*, and it applies only to Simon Peter. So are we out of luck?

Of course we're not. As Jesus walked from the Last Supper to the garden of Gethsemane, Peter heard him say this prayer:

> "I do not ask for these only, but also for those who will believe in me through their word. . . . Father, I desire that they also, whom you have given me, may be with me where I am, to see my glory that you have given me because you loved me before the foundation of the world. (John 17:20, 24)

Even today, some two thousand years later, Jesus is at the right hand of God praying for you. He lives to make intercession for you and appears before the Father on your behalf. Right this minute, wherever you are and whatever you're going through, Jesus is praying for you.

Like Peter, we can cross the line from darkness to light, from death to life, from Before to After, because of what Jesus has done for us. If we try to cross the line using our own strength and strategies, we will be sorely disappointed and severely wounded. The chasm is too deep, the wall is too high, the contrast is too great. Your willpower is too weak, your try-hard tendencies don't even toe the line. Your hopefulness is futile unless you hope fully in Christ. There is only one way to cross the line, and that is by his cross (did you notice the cross in the before-and-after diagrams in this chapter?). By his wounds we have been healed of our sin and our shame, and by his Spirit we prevail.

Peter's three denials are recorded in all four Gospels for all to see for all time, yet they are never mentioned again. He experienced healing in a tangible way as Jesus made him breakfast by the Sea of Galilee, and Peter promises that the same reprieve and restoration is available to you and to me:

> And after you have suffered a little while, the God of all grace,
> who has called you to his eternal glory in Christ, will himself
> restore, confirm, strengthen, and establish you. (1 Peter 5:10)

You can view change as the end of the world, or you can change your worldview. God's unchanging character promises your suffering will only last "a little while" on his eternal timeline. You have been chosen for this, and you can handle it with God's help. God himself will mend what has been broken. He will place you back on a firm foundation. He will make you strong where you are weak. He will put you back on your feet that he's even willing to wash. After your grief comes his glory.

When we have the same way of thinking as Jesus during our demolition, we will be reconstructed by God's grace. Peter closed this chapter about the theme of contrast with this instruction:

> Therefore let those who *suffer according to God's will* entrust their souls to a faithful Creator while doing good. (1 Peter 4:19)

It is God's will that we willingly suffer so that we will become like Christ. You can trust your faithful Creator's plans. You can confidently allow the Holy Spirit to bend and stretch you until your will mirrors his own. You can declare Jesus to be the Christ, Son of the living God, and hold up the blueprint of his life, death, and resurrection as the model for your own.

Peter knew his sin had nailed his Savior to the cross—and our sin did the same.

Peter saw love in Jesus's face even as he was betrayed—and he looks the same way at us.

Peter knew he was specifically forgiven and perfectly restored—and so are we.

The darkness within Peter was lit with the flame of the Holy Spirit, and he would never be silent again—and neither shall we.

A SECOND CUP

God is described in three ways in Romans 2:4. Define them in your own words, or use a dictionary: *kind, forbearing, patient.*

If you could see Jesus looking at you during your sin, what expression do you imagine you'd see on his face? Compare this to how Jesus looked at Peter when they

met and at his betrayal. How could a look from Jesus lead us to repentance?

Knowing Jesus forgave Peter's past mistakes, Peter was able to move on. This type of transformation is described in Philippians 3:13–14. What is lurking in your past that haunts you, preventing you from pressing on? How does knowing that Jesus wants to restore you change your outlook?

What is Jesus doing now?

> **Romans 8:34**
> **Hebrews 7:25**
> **Hebrews 9:24**

What would you ask Jesus to pray for you today? How do his prayers help you set your hope fully on him?

What has exhausted you as you try to cross the line from your old self to your new self in your own strength? How are we assured throughout Scripture that the battle will be won? Consider Psalm 33:16–22 and Ephesians 6:10–18 in your response.

Pray that the Holy Spirit will intervene and assist you.

Dear heavenly Father, you are so good to me, even when I don't deserve your kindness. Help me to fully receive your grace and to extend it to others who are hurting.
In Jesus's name, amen.

Lesson 5

Sarah's Story

Read 1 Peter 4:1–5

THE REJECTION BEGAN BEFORE SHE was even born. When her biological father left her pregnant mother, he left a lasting hole in Sarah's heart. "I always wondered why he didn't want me. I thought that if he knew me, then he would want me, and it would change everything," she remembers. "In my mind he was my savior, and I was hoping and waiting for the day I could meet him, and then everything would be okay."

Sarah's earliest memory was being grabbed by her ponytail and thrown against a wall. Physical and psychological abuse weren't unusual in her dysfunctional home, and neither were alcohol and drug abuse. When she was in elementary school, her mother and adoptive father announced they were divorcing. Sarah locked herself in the bathroom with a butcher knife until they promised to keep the family together, but her mother left the family just a few days later. "I felt unloved, abandoned, and rejected. I started down a path of seeking anything and everything I could to numb those feelings and feel loved."

Her birth father showed up at her doorstep on her thirteenth birthday, but Sarah's dreams were shattered when their reunion didn't go how she had always imagined it would. "I had to take a DNA test because he was never convinced that I was really his," she states. "I felt like I didn't have a father."

Her mother eventually returned and married a wealthy businessman. "I was happy with my new stepfather because I saw his money as a way to get the freedom to pursue whatever I wanted," Sarah reflects, "but I learned that money doesn't make everything better." He was also a personal trainer. "When I realized how important the appearance of the female body was to men, I thought that's how I could be loved. I developed an eating disorder, started working out all the time, and abused prescription drugs."

From there, her life slid downhill. "I tried to run away countless times. I cut myself. I wanted to die. I was addicted to alcohol and Adderall and had alcohol poisoning twice. I became sexually promiscuous at the age of twelve. I had an abortion as a teenager," Sarah recounts, listing these horrendous events as if they were childhood sports tournaments. "Three or four separate times, I was in jail, and I was expelled from school. I lived out of friends' homes and at one point lived in a car for several weeks."

For years, Sarah lived in hopeless darkness. Her grandmother took her to church and spent countless hours speaking spiritual wisdom over her, but Sarah didn't feel she knew how to live for God. "I saw a vision of Jesus when I was a child," she remembers. "I was paralyzed in that moment and can still see it perfectly in my mind. I now realize that this vision taught me the fear of the Lord." She made a promise that she would follow him later, perhaps when she was older.

"I was stuck in the mire of my sin," Sarah explains. "Satan deceived me into believing that the only way I could be loved and wanted was to be sexually immoral. I didn't think I could live any other way, and I had no idea how to cope with all the feelings I numbed every day or how to fix the problems in my life. I knew the way I was living was wrong, and I was overcome with guilt and shame. I thought God would be angry at me, and so I hid from him."

Sarah found herself pregnant again at age nineteen—but this time she married the baby's father. Her pregnancy was the first time she'd been sober since she was thirteen. "We were two broken and hurting people," Sarah says. She described her relationship as "either intoxicating and filled with lust, or toxic and abusive. There was no emotional or spiritual element." Police were frequently called to break up their fighting, and she began using drugs nearly every day again.

Sarah's life spiraled out of control, and she hit rock bottom when her grandmother threatened to take her daughter away. "I was bringing my child into the same dysfunction I had grown up in," she realized, "and she was also going to end up motherless and fatherless if I didn't do something." Completely lost, broken, and hopeless, dead in immorality and darkness, Sarah desperately wanted to change. Lying facedown on the bathroom floor, more than a little hungover, Sarah remembers, "I felt hands grabbing my arms and legs, pulling me down—and I knew that hell was trying to suck me in."

True sorrow flooded the depths of her soul, and she finally cried out to God. Sarah had tried everything to fill the void in her heart and bring her peace—everything except Jesus. She was finally ready to give him the chance she had always promised.

Raising her hands in full surrender, she got on her knees and prayed, "Jesus, if you will show me that you're real and you love me and forgive me, I promise I will live every day for the rest of my life for you." She asked the Lord to give her a son whom she could raise to love God. "In that moment, I felt warmth wash over my body. The peace I had been longing for my whole life filled my heart, and I never looked back. My son was born exactly nine months later."

Sarah practically used 1 Peter 4:3 as a checklist in her old life:

For the time that is past suffices for doing what the Gentiles
want to do, living in sensuality, passions, drunkenness, orgies,
drinking parties, and lawless idolatry. (1 Peter 4:3)

But now that she was determined to walk with God, the following
verse was also fulfilled:

With respect to this they are surprised when you do not join
them in the same flood of debauchery, and they malign you.
(1 Peter 4:4)

The closer she drew to the Lord, the further a wedge was driven
into her marriage, until a revelation of repeated infidelity destroyed
her vision of a happy ending. Despite her worst fears coming true, she
was excited for a fresh start as she and her husband sought counseling
together at the church she'd been attending. "I was so hopeful that the
Lord would restore my marriage. I wanted my testimony to be like the
couples in the marriage reconciliation program. I wanted to help others
who were hurting with the story of how God redeemed us."

But soon Sarah found herself sitting alone at the sessions, and ten-
sions rose at home as she no longer did the things she used to do. "He
even sent me a song called 'She Left Me for Jesus.' But I didn't leave,
despite counsel from my pastors and strong Christian friends. I had no
peace about leaving and didn't want to have any regrets. I wanted to
give it my all and do everything I possibly could to save my marriage.
My faith was sorely tested."

Looking back at her journals from that time, the pain is fresh. "I'm
really struggling, Lord," she wrote. "I feel so unlovable and abandoned."
The teaching her grandmother had poured into her now poured itself
out on the page. "I know you have a purpose and a plan for me. You are
for me, not against me. You will uphold me with your righteous right
hand. You keep all my tears in a bottle. You love me, you adore me.

Please comfort me. Please show me what to do. Take care of me. Please heal my heart. I'm scared of the future. Help me trust you more. Bring me closer to you. Fill me with your Spirit. Let me see the light ahead and not the darkness behind me."

She and the children were kicked out of their home, and the marriage ended. "I had nothing. I was a single mom with no car, no job, no college education. I didn't even have anyone to watch my infant and toddler so I could get a job. But the Lord came through for me in mighty, huge ways. He taught me to trust in him with all my heart and lean not on my own understanding. As I acknowledged him in all my ways, he literally directed every step of the way" (Proverbs 3:5–6). Sarah's face lights up as she remembers those difficult times. "There were times I couldn't pay my bills if I tithed, but I felt this was an important step of faith. When I gave, he gave more. I learned so much through those trials."

Sarah was working in an environment where there was drinking in the office and after hours. She was tormented by her boss and coworkers for not going along as she used to, but she had confidence that she had been placed there for two reasons: to be a light in the darkness and to strengthen her faith. "You can't have one foot in the world and one foot following the Lord," Sarah advises. "He tells us to flee immorality, so you have to make a decision."

Even as she made conscious decisions about how she wanted to live, Sarah was shocked when her grandmother encouraged her to wait until she remarried to be intimate with a man again. "That had always been such an important part of my life," Sarah recalls. "I had not thought about that part of Christianity and my walk with the Lord before, and honestly, I was really mad at her for bringing that to my attention!" As she prayed about it—already knowing the answer—she asked the Lord to help her want to do his will. "He gently and patiently changed my heart, and I decided to stay pure for him." Her prayers were straight from Scripture:

> Live for the rest of the time in the flesh no longer for human passions but for the will of God. (1 Peter 4:2)

This is about the time when I met Sarah. Actually, I met her grandmother, who is my neighbor, mentor, and dear friend. When Debbie requested intercession for her granddaughter, a circle of godly women asked God to strengthen Sarah's faith and hold her close.

Making decisions that aligned with her new faith brought purity and pain as she stepped even deeper into the suffering she was already experiencing. Sarah describes the suffering as "both emotional and physical. I encountered temptation, and that was hard. I struggled every day, but God gave me grace to endure. 1 Peter 4:1 says that whoever has suffered in the flesh has ceased from sin, and that's exactly what I experienced. I had to let the Lord retrain me from seeking approval and validation from a man, to seeing my worth in God's eyes, and getting my comfort from him." That verse reads:

> Since therefore Christ suffered in the flesh, arm yourselves with the same way of thinking, for whoever has suffered in the flesh has ceased from sin. (1 Peter 4:1)

Following God's will instead of our own isn't easy, but it is worthy. Sarah cautions, "Dying to yourself daily is a painful process. Putting off the old and putting on the new is hard work." She looked to verses like Romans 5:3–5 and James 1:2–4 that show the path from suffering to endurance to hope and maturity. "I learned to embrace the suffering, and the Lord used it to change me in ways I never thought possible," she says now with awe. When she surrendered to the painful process of stripping her old ways, God quickly stepped in and filled her heart with the grace and peace she longed for.

There were also moments of great joy, like when she was baptized by her Christian counselor. "Coming up out of the water, I felt the peace that passes understanding and inexplicable joy! I felt white as snow, and free—so free." At her counselor's suggestion, she began writing several verses from Proverbs in her own words daily so she could replace old ways of thinking with God's truth. She paid special attention to the emotional, physical, relational, and financial consequences of living in immorality described in Proverbs 5–7, contrasted with the blessings of obedience in Proverbs 8 and Deuteronomy 28. "I wouldn't have known the truth unless I was in God's Word," Sarah remembers, a lesson we can all take to heart.

Relationships with her mother and biological father were restored, and for a while it seemed that her marriage would be, too. Seeing signs of repentance, Sarah remarried her ex-husband after six years apart; however, the reconciliation was short-lived and they divorced after two years. "I know I prayed that decision through; I know I was obedient to God and listened closely to his voice," Sarah says confidently. "I also know that my divorce was justified, as I confirmed through wise advice from my pastors and family. It took just as much trust, faith, and surrender to file for divorce as it did to get married." Sarah felt the disappointment of unfulfilled dreams even when she knew she was walking in the center of God's will.

Sarah relates deeply to the woman in Mark 5:25–34 who suffered debilitating pain and rejection for many years before she encountered Jesus. "That's exactly what my life felt like!" Sarah exclaims. "That woman was in so much pain for so many years, and no one could help her. I knew her desperation and hopelessness. My heart and soul felt like they were bleeding out of me before I met Jesus, too!"

Sarah tried to find happiness in what the world has to offer and was left empty, bruised, and aching. Jesus healed her heart and filled the void with love, joy, peace, and hope. "Sometimes I'll catch myself trying to take control and must remind myself to hope fully in God's grace," Sarah comments. "My hope is not in a man or a marriage; it's not in my career. Jesus alone is my hope, and he has never failed me.

"He won't fail you, either."

A SECOND CUP

 When have you been maligned (spoken poorly of) because of the choices you've made as a Christian? What sustains you through these times?

 Sarah paid a high price when she started following Jesus. What has your faith cost you? What would you be willing to give up to follow Jesus?

 Read 1 Peter 1–3 and 5 in your Bible, marking passages about the contrast between our old self and new self with a divided circle to remember your new life in Christ:

Dear heavenly Father, I'm willing to do whatever it takes to fully follow you. Please pry my fingers apart when I cling to my old ways, and replace all my desires with your good and perfect will. In Jesus's name, amen.

CHAPTER 5

HOW TO SURVIVE THE END OF THE WORLD

1 Peter 4:7–11

DIRE REPORTS FROM DOCTORS, SCIENTISTS, and government officials had been broadcast into our living rooms for months, warning us of looming social and economic disaster on a global scale. Now the moment of truth had arrived, and we perched anxiously on the edges of our sofas watching the drama unfold before our eyes. Our homes were full of food, water, gas, and cash (Lord knows we had plenty of toilet paper), and our hearts were full of fear.

But when Dick Clark shouted, "Five—four—three—two—ONE!" nothing happened.

Y2K fell from hype to a hangover when the ball dropped in Times Square. Lights stayed on, banks stayed open, and airplanes didn't fall from the sky; Jesus didn't even return as many had predicted. A collective sigh was heard around the world as we quickly returned to our normal routines. The best-laid plans often go awry, even disaster plans.

Then there are catastrophes we never see coming and have no time to pack a bag for, let alone buy food in bulk.

We've been working sequentially through each chapter of 1 Peter, but now we're going to hang out in 1 Peter 4:7–11 for a while. In these five verses, Peter provides five simple and effective coping strategies you can put on your to-do list and check off one by one the next time problems rain down faster than confetti on New Year's Eve.

When it all comes crashing down, we have no say-so over other people's behavior, the weather, who's in office, timelines and deadlines, financial pressures, global pandemics, and the like—but we *can* control how we react and respond. When you see a verse about something you can control in a crisis, draw a circle with a check mark, like this:

Peter never shies away from the painful reality in which we live. He begins this passage with an ominous warning that a TEOTWAWKI moment might be right around the corner:

> The end of the world is coming soon. Therefore . . . (1 Peter 4:7 NLT)

Of course, we must ask what the *therefore* is there for: it's the pivot Peter uses to swing from scary predictions to practical steps. Whether "the end" is the Second Coming or the first day you wake up in a world that looks nothing like you planned, you can stand firm on these rock-solid end-time strategies as Jesus's grace and glory are revealed.

Predictably, Peter utterly failed to follow his own strategies before he became our go-to guy for how-to tips. He learned these tactics from watching Jesus, and we'll learn from both of them how to survive the end of the world.

 Scan this code or visit www.amylively.com/cup-of-hope /#chapter5 to access online resources and read the Scripture passages online.

——— ✦ ———

Pray Mindfully

Read 1 Peter 4:7, Mark 4:35–41, and Matthew 14:22–33

WHEN YOUR WORLD FALLS APART, you want answers fast. So in a traumatic year like 2020, is it any wonder that Bible sales skyrocketed and "how to pray" trended in Google searches?[1] This search term spiked to its all-time high during the Las Vegas shooting and peaked again when Russia invaded Ukraine. On my website, the most popular page is about how to pray for our neighbors. We want to know how to speak so that God will listen—or how to listen so that God will speak. And okay, I'll admit it, I want to know how to pray so that I get results.

Peter, the same guy who repeatedly fell asleep when Jesus specifically asked him to stay awake and pray, taught that we should pray with our mind fully focused on God and our hope fully set on his grace. This is our first surprising strategy for surviving our TEOTWAWKI moments:

> The end of the world is coming soon. Therefore, be earnest and disciplined in your prayers. (1 Peter 4:7 NLT)

The two words Peter uses to describe our mindset during prayer—earnest and disciplined in the New Living Translation—are interpreted as self-controlled, sober-minded, alert, wide-awake (love that one!), clearheaded, reasonable, specific, focused, balanced, serious, and watchful in other various translations. This type of prayer isn't overwhelmed or controlled by strong emotions, and it considers all sides of a situation.

We learn to pray by observing Jesus. Peter and the other disciples knew he had special places where he went to pray at all hours of the night and day. They had seen him pray on mountaintops, in homes, at gravesides, and in the temple. They waited as Jesus went away to pray alone and watched him pray in crowds. Jesus prayed with adults and children. He prayed for people and about people, and he prayed for himself. He made petitions and offered praise; he prayed when he was joyous and when he was distressed.

When the disciples asked Jesus to teach them how to pray, he responded with what is commonly called The Lord's Prayer. It's the most frequently recited prayer to this day, and most English-speaking people say it in the old King James language. Jesus told them to pray like this:

> "Our Father which art in heaven, Hallowed be thy name. Thy kingdom come, Thy will be done in earth, as it is in heaven. Give us this day our daily bread. And forgive us our debts, as we forgive our debtors. And lead us not into temptation, but deliver us from evil: For thine is the kingdom, and the power, and the glory, for ever. Amen." (Matthew 6:9–13 KJV)

Early Christians recited the Lord's Prayer at nine o'clock in the morning, at noon, and again at three o'clock in the afternoon;[2] church bells used to ring throughout the day to remind the faithful to say these words. It's a beautiful prayer that probably served as the standard for Peter's "prayer test" of earnestness and discipline, and we should meditate upon it often, keeping our minds fully engaged so that our prayers don't become meaningless.

We may use beautiful prayers like this to guide us, and we are also invited to use our own words as we pour out our hearts to our Father. One of my favorite things about Christian prayer is that we can do it anytime, anywhere, any way. We can pray standing up or sitting down, in the shower or driving a car. You can sing or dance while you pray. There is no gesture we must make, no direction we must face, no schedule we must keep. If you're going to pray without ceasing, as we're told in Scripture (1 Thessalonians 5:17), you'll need to pray with your eyes open and closed, your hands folded, and raised, and chopping vegetables at the kitchen sink. We have so much freedom in our prayers! It would almost be easier if Jesus had given us a formula or checklist guaranteed to get results, but he is more interested in a personal conversation.

How to P.R.A.Y.

Jesus didn't dictate rigid prayer formulas; he gave us flexible prayer models. We can incorporate prayer patterns into our daily dialogue with God:

P = Position

Jesus began the Lord's Prayer by positioning us under the authority, care, and provision of our Father in heaven. We're even encouraged to call God our "Abba, Father," a pairing of words that together imply intimacy and reverence. (I was surprised to learn that *abba* does not mean "daddy" as I'd always believed. This definition was popularized in the 1970s when a theologian suggested the word sounded like a babbling child—*abba . . . dada . . . papa . . .* It kinda makes sense. Even though he recanted this definition, the teaching stuck.[3]) *Abba* is a title used by children and adults to convey family familiarity, submission to authority, and respectful willingness to obey. When we call our Father *Abba*, we are praying from a position of trust, a place of safety, a posture of humility.

R = Reverence

Jesus acknowledged our Father's power when he told us to pray, "hallowed be thy name." Be honest: when was the last time you used *hallowed* in a sentence? We don't often use this word that means holy, revered, and sacred. But when we include praise, worship, thanksgiving, and adoration in our prayers, we remember that our hallowed God can do anything and everything we need.

A = Ask

Jesus teaches us to plainly ask for what we need. God stands ready to provide our needs for each day, forgive our misdeeds, and shield us from trouble. Do you need healing from sickness, escape from addiction, relief from financial pressures, or restoration in relationships? Ask, and see.

Y = Yield

Jesus shows us how to leave our prayers in God's hands with the words, "Thy kingdom come, Thy will be done, on earth as it is in heaven. . . . For thine is the kingdom, and the power, and the glory, for ever." When I feel overwhelmed and under-equipped to deal with the weight of the world, this prayer pattern reminds me that God alone is the keeper of his kingdom. He brings people and problems and even praises into our lives so that we can return them back to him, giving him all glory— and responsibility.

There's another prayer pattern you've heard so many times you may have stopped hearing it: "In Jesus's name, amen." Let's set our minds fully on this common way to end a prayer instead of saying it mechanically. The meaning became clear to me when I helped my father-in-law with a legal document. Instead of driving to his attorney's office to sign the paper, he asked that it be emailed to me. Since my father-in-law trusted me and was familiar with the document, he asked me to print and sign it "in his name" before sending it back. My aha moment came as I signed his name on the signature line: a prayer "in Jesus's name" is as if Jesus himself is signing off on our words to our Father.

Amen has been called the most widely recognized word in every language. This word originated in the Hebrew Bible, and its pronunciation remained the same in the Greek language of the New Testament and languages around the world today. At the end of a prayer, *amen* means "so be it" or "may it be so." Taken together, "in Jesus's name, amen" means that we are signing his name on our prayers; we want our words to sound like his voice and our wishes to align with his will. Saying "in Jesus's name, amen" at the end of a prayer doesn't stamp his approval on our prayer; rather, it signals our acceptance of his reply.

Water-Walking Prayers

When Peter found himself in desperate situations where he needed God to quickly intervene, he didn't have time to shout, "My-Father-which-art-in-heaven-hallowed-be-thy-name-give-me-my-daily-bread-in-Jesus's-name-amen!" Let's go to the Mark 4:35–41 scene at the Sea of Galilee, which was a familiar body of water to Peter. He had probably known fishermen who had perished in its sudden, violent squalls like the one that was flooding the disciples' boat that night. As they bailed water from the bow, Jesus slept comfortably on a cushion in the stern.

You've been in that boat, sailing peacefully along until a sudden gale force threatens to destroy what you love, and waves crash over the sides of your watertight life. You understand what the disciples meant when they finally managed to wake Jesus from his nap: "Teacher, do you not care that we are perishing?" What are you doing? Why aren't you helping? Do you not see the trouble I'm in? Could you at least grab a bucket? God can handle your frustrated, fist-shaking prayers.

Jesus awoke and did so much more than dip a little water from the boat. He spoke to the wind and said to the sea, "Peace! Be still!" In an instant, the destructive storm ceased, and a palpable stillness settled over the shivering crew. "Why are you so afraid?" he asked. "Have you still no faith?"

Not long after, Peter found himself tossed about on the stormy Sea of Galilee once again. Miles from shore, rowing hard against a fierce wind and battered by waves, Peter and the disciples peered into the rough sea and saw a ghost walking on the water toward their boat! As they cried out in fear, immediately they heard the voice of Jesus call out, "Take heart; it is I. Do not be afraid." Peter uttered his first prayer in the storm:

> "Lord, if it be thou, bid me come unto thee on the water."
> Matthew 14:28 (KJV)

Big storms call for King James prayers! Jesus didn't stop the wind or calm the waves or change the weather or rebuke the circumstances—he invited Peter into the miracle in the mayhem. Which is the greater miracle: calming the sea or carrying the sailor? Jesus can do both! In my experience, Jesus is more likely to hold your hand as you walk on water than wave his hand and settle your storm.

Peter boldly asked if he could join Jesus in the storm, and at Jesus's word, Peter got out of the boat and walked on the water. I wonder how many steps Peter took before he sank. Three steps? Fifty? It wasn't a wave that overpowered him, and he didn't sink because of the severity of the storm. Peter began to sink when he took his eyes off Jesus:

> But when he saw the wind, he was afraid, and beginning to sink he cried out, "Lord, save me." Jesus immediately reached out his hand and took hold of him, saying to him, "O you of little faith, why did you doubt?" (Matthew 14:30–31)

You can't "see" wind. You can only see the effect of wind. Peter looked at the storm-tossed waves instead of Jesus standing beside him. He heard howling in his ears instead of Jesus's command to come, and the spray hitting his face felt more substantial than the water beneath his feet. Peter's doubt and fear became more real to him than what was actually happening: he was walking on waves with Jesus! The same Spirit who hovered over the water at creation (Genesis 1:2) was walking with Peter on the Sea of Galilee.

Slipping beneath the water, Peter cried out, "Lord, save me!" and Jesus reached out and answered Peter's prayer as the words left his lips. This is the only prayer you need when you are storm tossed and scared. "Lord, save me!" properly positions God as Lord and reveres him as Savior, plainly asks for the urgent need, and yields to his firm grip in the storm.

When Jesus rescued Peter, he said, "O you of *little* faith," but in the first storm Jesus said the disciples had "*no* faith." A *little* faith is all that's needed to pray. Little-faith prayers release God's water-walking power.

The Prayer That Never Fails

Scripture abounds with prayers from kings like David, shepherds like Moses, prophets like Isaiah, apostles like Paul, barren women like Hannah, and distraught mothers like Mary. There are prayers from the depths of the sea like Jonah, and cries from the crest of the waves like Peter. Of all the prayers recorded on the pages of our Bibles, there is one that sums up all the others, a one-size-fits-all prayer perfectly suited for every problem any one of us will ever face. This is a prayer that never fails, a wish God must always grant.

This prayer is simple, but it's not easy; in fact, it may be the most difficult prayer you'll ever utter. It certainly was for Jesus. He gave us these words just days before his crucifixion during what we have come to call Holy Week. He knew what was coming. He was prepared for the suffering. He anticipated the pain, awaited the betrayal. His soul was troubled but steadfast when he said these words:

"Father, glorify your name." (John 12:28)

This isn't a make-it-go-away prayer; it's a sustain-me-through-the-pain prayer. In our darkest hours and hardest trials, this is a prayer to which God will always answer, "Yes!" He will equip you, help you, hold you, lead you, comfort you, bless you, and keep you through your tears and fears when your heart's desire is to glorify his name. This prayer shifts our gaze from our earthly problems to our heavenly Father's face, from our situation to his salvation, from any selfish ambition or self-help solution to his glory, goodness, and grace. This prayer asks God to redeem our painful moments and use every test of our faith and trial of our heart to testify to his praise. This prayer releases every outcome into his capable hands. It helps us lay down our rights and sacrifice ourselves, just like Jesus did. When we seek God's glory in our story, our prayers will always get results.

When you're losing your mind, prayer helps you keep your head. And when you come to your own end times—the end of a dream, the end of yourself—earnest and disciplined prayer will bring God's presence, peace, and power into your storm.

Can I get an amen?

A SECOND CUP

 Where were you on December 31, 1999? What do you remember about Y2K? If that's before your time, share about a situation when you tried to be prepared but something entirely unexpected happened.

Study Jesus's prayer habits in these verses. When, where, and how did Jesus pray?

> Matthew 14:23
> Mark 1:35
> Luke 5:16

When, where, and how do you pray?

 God's Word offers suggestions (not commandments) about our physical posture while we pray. Note how Jesus engaged his entire body in prayer.

> His eyes in John 11:41
> His hands in Luke 24:50
> On his knees in Mark 14:35
> At the table in Luke 24:30

Try a new posture and see if it helps your mind engage in prayer.

 Peter wrote that we should cast all our cares on God because he cares for us (1 Peter 5:7). Use the P.R.A.Y. method to cast a care in prayer. Bonus: do it King James style and write a bold, water-walking prayer.

 Post the prayer that never fails—"Father, glorify your name!"—in your home where you can see it often. How does this prayer shift your current prayer requests?

Visit www.amylively.com/pray for a free printable prayer guide based on Scripture, or scan this code:

Dear heavenly Father, please show me where you are in my storms. Take my hand and help me walk above the mayhem so that my story brings you praise and glory. In Jesus's name, amen.

Lesson 2

— ❊ —

Love Soulfully

Read 1 Peter 4:8, 1 Corinthians 13:4–7, and Acts 10

WE USE THE WORD *LOVE* loosely, don't we? I know I do. I love my husband. I love peanut butter. I love my dog. I love my daughter. I love my root-lifter spray mousse. The New Testament was written in the Greek language, which has four words we translate into English as *love*:[4]

- *Eros* (*eer*-os): intimate love, attraction, sexual desire. Eros was the Greek god of love. Root of the word *erotic*.
- *Storge* (*stor*-ghee): natural or instinctual affection such as that felt by parents for offspring. Used almost exclusively for family relationships.
- *Philia* (fil-*eh*-ah): camaraderie, friendship, affectionate love, including loyalty to friends, family, and community. Root of the word *Philadelphia*, City of Brotherly Love. Opposite of *phobia* or *fear*.
- *Agape* (ag-*ah*-pay): unconditional love, to love dearly. Sacrificial love. Good will and affection, benevolence, compassion.

The words *eros* and *storge* are not used in the Bible, but *agape* and *philia* are used hundreds of times. *Agape* love is a Christian concept that was rarely used in ancient manuscripts prior to the writing of the New Testament.[5] John 3:16 is about agape love:

> For God so loved the world, that he gave his only Son, that whoever believes in him should not perish but have eternal life. (John 3:16)

This is the kind of love Peter had in mind when he wrote the most important survival strategy, what I'm calling "love soulfully":

> Most important of all, continue to show deep love for each other, for love covers a multitude of sins. (1 Peter 4:8 NLT)

When Peter talks about *deep* love, he's not talking about your average, ordinary love; this is earnest love, unfailing, fervent love. The root word of deep is *ekteinō* (ek-*ti*-no), which means to stretch out or extend something, such as your hand. God loved us so much that he stretched out his hand and gave us his Son. Jesus loved us so much that he stretched out his arms to be nailed to the cross.

You guessed it: Peter is calling us to *agape* love, the kind of love that reaches out and gives something precious of itself. This kind of love is unconditional, unceasing, unwavering, and unrelenting. It's undeserved. It's uncomfortable love, the kind of love that stretches your heart to the breaking point as your soul loves fully.

This kind of love will cost you something.

This kind of love is a side effect of salvation, Peter explained:

> You were cleansed from your sins when you obeyed the truth, so now you must show sincere love [*philia*] to each other as

brothers and sisters. Love [*agape*] each other deeply with all your heart. (1 Peter 1:22 NLT)

Peter covers *all* the love bases, from familial love to unfailing love, with *agape*. So what would it look like if all God's people deeply, sincerely, and earnestly loved others? What is that love, and where do we find it?

The Most Important Command

Peter knew what Jesus taught about love. He remembered when a sect of legalistic Jews called Pharisees tried to test Jesus by asking him to pick the most important commandment in the Old Testament. The Pharisees loved their laws; in fact, they had counted 613 of them in the first five books of the Bible known as the Torah. I wonder if the Pharisees hoped Jesus would royally mess up and pick one of these laws:[6]

Law #52
Don't plant a tree in the Temple courtyard (Deuteronomy 16:21).

Law #186
Don't eat worms found in fruit on the ground (Leviticus 11:42).

Law #605
Build your latrine outside your camp (Deuteronomy 23:13).

Instead, Jesus replied:

"You shall love the Lord your God with all your heart and with all your soul and with all your mind. This is the great and first commandment. And a second is like it: You shall love your neighbor as yourself." (Matthew 22:37–39)

The Pharisees were more concerned with obeying laws than loving people. They loved religious rules more than real relationships and would rather point an accusing finger than stretch out a helping hand. Jesus changed the game when he named love—unquantifiable, imprecise, unconditional love—as the most important law.

I once rented a car during a speaking engagement in Dallas. When my GPS pointed me toward a toll road, I carefully followed its directions so I wouldn't get lost on the complex freeway (it didn't matter, I got lost anyway). Several weeks later I received a letter from the car rental company, which I assumed was a loyalty reward or coupon for my next rental. Instead, they charged my credit card for the $2 toll . . . along with a $25 penalty. I certainly don't expect my car rental company to love me unconditionally, and I should have known the rules. But it made me realize that I tend to love others in the same way: "I love you until you break one of my rules, then BAM! I'll slap you with a penalty." I love you *if* you follow the rules, *if* you think like me, *if* you do what I say, *if* you love me back. Jesus changes the game and raises the stakes:

> If you love those who love you, what benefit is that to you? For even sinners love those who love them. (Luke 6:32)

Loving the lovely is easy. It's the unlovely people who challenge us to move from "Love *if* . . ." to "Love *is* . . ."

Love *If* or Love *Is*

The next four verses are some of the most thought-provoking, irritating, and meddlesome verses in the entire Bible:

> Love is patient and kind; love does not envy or boast; it is not arrogant or rude. It does not insist on its own way; it is not

irritable or resentful; it does not rejoice at wrongdoing, but rejoices with the truth. Love bears all things, believes all things, hopes all things, endures all things. (1 Corinthians 13:4–7)

Since "God is love" (1 John 4:8, 16), we can substitute his name in this passage easily—"God is patient and kind. God is not jealous or boastful . . ." Yeah, that works. And since we're supposed to be imitators of God (Ephesians 5:1), let's stick our name in those verses in the love chapter. "Amy is patient and kind; Amy does not envy or boast; Amy is not arrogant or rude. Amy does not insist on her own way; Amy is not irritable or resentful . . ."

Well, we can just stop right there. It's a nice goal, but it's not my reality—just ask my family. I can't simply set my mind to it and make it happen. I can't act that way toward the people I do truly love, and I certainly can't do it for the unlovable. How in the world can I imitate the *agape* love of Christ?

There is no way in the world you can muster up Christ's kind of love—and that, friends, is the best news ever! This love comes from outside us, an infusion of the Holy Spirit that transforms your heart from unkind, impatient, rude, and cranky to joyful, generous, kind, and hopeful. God doesn't expect us to manufacture a little bit of love. He doesn't give us an impossible command to "go love everyone" and then leave us unprepared. The love he commands from us he will also pour into us! This is how he equips us to love soulfully.

The Holy Spirit gives us love for others. God himself is our teacher, the one who demonstrates and educates us in Loving 101. The Lord will give us love, make it grow, and teach us how to love well. He did this for Peter, and he can do it for us, too.

There is a learning curve to love, so let's look at two stories about Peter that show his slow progress in acquiring this new skill.

The Best

As a Jew, Peter adhered to extremely strict dietary laws that forbade eating or even touching certain foods. In Acts 10 we read that as Peter prayed, he had a vision of a large sheet being let down from heaven (I can't help but wonder if this was the author's attempt at describing an IMAX screen!). Animals, reptiles and birds filled the sheet and a voice told Peter to kill and eat them. Three times, Peter refused to eat the animals because they were ceremoniously unclean and impure. Each time, the voice said, "Do not call something unclean if God has made it clean."

For Peter to eat these animals would be as disgusting as serving buzzard at your Thanksgiving dinner. It was stomach-turning, gut-wrenching, and gross.

Unfortunately, Peter saw people the same way. Peter wasn't permitted to share a meal with anyone who was not a Jew. He couldn't enter Gentiles' homes, be their friends, or worship with them. It made that whole "go and make disciples" thing a little difficult, and Peter continually struggled with acceptance of those who weren't born into the Jewish faith. This vision in Acts wasn't about food but fellowship.

Immediately after this vision, Peter was asked to visit the home of a Roman centurion. Centurions were the soldiers who crucified Christ. They commanded armies, defended emperors, and regularly killed people. Centurions were feared by their enemies and friends—and now one of them was inviting Peter for dinner! What could he say, except:

> "You know it is against our laws for a Jewish man to enter a Gentile home like this or to associate with you. But God has shown me that I should no longer think of anyone as impure or unclean." (Acts 10:28 NLT)

As much as you might try to convince yourself that you're open-minded and accepting, a glance around the sanctuary, or your Facebook friends, or your neighborhood will probably reveal that people look a lot like you. When someone walks in who looks, believes, or behaves differently, we raise our eyebrows, curl our lips, and move our seats. Worse, we close our mouths and don't speak up when we see injustice, racism, discrimination, and plain ol' hatred.

We're not that different from Peter after all.

Agape love is content with people as they are, no strings attached, no hoops to jump through. *Agape* love doesn't always affirm everyone's choices, but it is patient, kind, and gentle when we don't agree. *Agape* love elevates others ahead of our ourselves, then leaves the consequences up to God. *Agape* love looks beyond external differences to a person's heart. *Agape* love like Jesus's embraces, defends, and protects every soul. If a quarrelsome, prideful, and prejudiced man like Peter was transformed by the power of God into a peaceful, accepting, and loving person, then there is certainly hope for us!

Some days my heart feels hard and thick, unmalleable and immovable; other times, I'm stretched so thin that one more act of love feels like it will split me in two. These are the moments when God can flood our hearts with so much love that we have some to spare. He will hold your hand as you reach out to love others who are unlike you, teaching you how to love recklessly and soulfully, leaving the consequences to him.

A SECOND CUP

 Since we can't go to the Love Store and pick up a few more gallons, where can we get more love?

Romans 5:5
Colossians 1:8 (NLT)
1 Thessalonians 3:12
1 Thessalonians 4:9

How does knowing that love comes from outside of ourselves give us hope?

 Jesus took the Golden Rule and kicked it up a notch. Compare these verses:

What is the basis for love in Matthew 7:12?
What is the condition for love in Luke 6:32?
Who sets the standard for loving others in John 13:34?
How would the world be transformed if we loved like Jesus regardless of what we wanted or how others behaved?

 Draw a picture or diagram of the progression from suffering to our experience of God's love as explained in Romans 5:3–5. How have you experienced God's love and the Holy Spirit's presence during a hard situation?

 There's also a connection between forgiveness and love. Read Luke 7:41–47. How did the forgiveness Peter received affect his ability to love others? Why must we constantly recognize our need for forgiveness to love others well?

Dear heavenly Father, some days I'm running short on love. You created love, you embody love, and you freely give love. Please fill me up with your love so I can pour it out to others. In Jesus's name, amen.

Lesson 3

— ❊ —

Share Cheerfully

Read 1 Peter 4:9 and Mark 6:30–44

THERE ARE VERY REAL AND life-threatening emergencies happening in the homes you drive by in your neighborhood each day:

> *Mom isn't eating, and Dad can't remember my name. How will I take care of them?*
>
> *Stage 4. I wonder if I'll be in a lot of pain. What will I look like without eyebrows?*
>
> *He says he loves her. Will he leave me? What about the kids?*
>
> *She hasn't called for three days. Is she on another binge?*
>
> *Should I pay the phone bill or the electric bill? I definitely can't make the rent.*
>
> *I'm so lonely. Would anyone miss me if I were gone?*

These are the people Peter had in mind when he wrote our next survival strategy: share cheerfully. Consider this verse:

The end of the world is coming soon. Therefore . . . cheerfully

share your home with those who need a meal or a place to stay.
(1 Peter 4:7, 9 NLT)

Even before the pandemic, your neighborhood was experiencing a deadly epidemic of loneliness. Millions of our neighbors were already socially isolated with few friends and little personal contact or communication, leading to loneliness that etches itself into our DNA and physically alters the brain. As I learned when I wrote *How to Love Your Neighbor Without Being Weird*:

> Lonely people are more likely to be obese and experience memory loss, dementia, inflammation, depression, sleep disorders, and heart conditions. Lonely people are less likely to exercise or survive surgery. Loneliness increases levels of stress hormones. It impacts how long we live and how often we are sick.[7]

Loneliness, domestic violence, child abuse, substance abuse, anxiety disorders, depression, anger, insomnia, and suicide are on the increase and are only expected to rise,[8] aided and abetted by the pandemic, economic uncertainty, job insecurity, social discord, and political upheaval. For TEOTWAWKI seasons like this, Peter's command is that we show hospitality to one another.

This end-time strategy is simple: be nice to strangers. The people Peter refers to as exiles, sojourners, aliens, or foreigners—who you might think are the guests who should receive kindness—are the ones commanded to show friendliness. We are never such a friend of God as when we are being friendly to one another.

When I moved to the middle of nowhere, knowing no one, to a tiny little town I had only visited one time, God sent three special women to show me hospitality. They made me feel welcome, introduced me to more friends, took me to church, and gave me the inside scoop on doctors and hairdressers. Have you been on the receiving end of this kind of kindness? If you have, you'll never forget how its perfect timing sparked a twinge of hope in your heart. Or have you ever had an inexplicable nudge to reach out to someone—an old friend you haven't seen for far too long or an acquaintance you met only briefly? God could be trying to use you as his special messenger. Your text or call could come at just the right moment to let someone know God has not forgotten them. This is the secret of hospitality and the brilliance of this command.

The Secret Ingredient

Peter's secret ingredient is *cheerfulness*, a quality I sometimes sorely lack because, let's face it, hospitality can be hard. If you've ever been invited to someone's home only to have them fuss and fret over the food or gripe about how hard it was to get ready, you know that kind of behavior doesn't exactly make for a comfortable or welcoming visit. We can have meaningful conversations in messy rooms. To share cheerfully means without grumbling or complaining and without making the whole family miserable. It doesn't mean you have to scrub the baseboards, fold your napkins like a swan, or make a gourmet meal.

Perhaps Peter learned this strategy when he helped Jesus serve dinner to a few thousand guests. In typical Peter fashion, we'll see him mess things up himself before he can write them down for us. The story of Jesus feeding five thousand men (not even counting women and children) is found in all four Gospels (Matthew 14, Mark 6, Luke 9, John 6). Mark, a close friend and traveling companion of Peter, gives the backstory for this miraculous meal.

Jesus was becoming more popular by the day. In Mark 6, we read that he was healing the sick, casting out demons, preaching with authority, resurrecting the dead, even taming the weather. As people heard about all he was doing, crowds began to follow him wherever he went. In his personal life, he was grieving for his dear friend and relative John the Baptist, who had been brutally murdered.

People were pressed in on him from every side, wanting to touch him, demanding his attention—wanting him to fix all their problems.

Does this sound like your life? You young parents who can't even go to the bathroom alone, Jesus knows how you feel! When you come home from a long day at work and your work at home is only just beginning, Jesus understands how you feel. When the demands of your life exceed the energy in your bones, Jesus knows how you feel. Jesus did everything for his disciples: he taught them, trained them, guided them, loved them, provided for them—not only them, but the multitudes tagging along. As Jesus tried to get away with his disciples to find a quiet place to rest, the crowds just kept pushing in. He had no time to eat, let alone pray or rest.

You could say Jesus was having a bad day.

And that's okay. We all have bad days. Most of us, however, have a bad response to a bad day—but not Jesus. He stopped. He looked into his neighbors' eyes and was moved with compassion. He saw people who were lost, directionless, searching. He sat with them and poured himself into them. Late in the afternoon, Peter and the disciples came to him and said:

> "This is a remote place, and it's already getting late. Send the crowds away so they can go to the nearby farms and villages and buy something to eat." (Mark 6:35–36 NLT)

I love the disciples' idea of compassion: let's send the people away so they can fend for themselves! Jesus would have none of it:

> But Jesus said, "You feed them."
> "With what?" they asked. "We'd have to work for months to earn enough money to buy food for all these people!" (Mark 6:37 NLT)

Somehow, they managed to round up five loaves of bread and two measly fish. Jesus took their little offering, looked to heaven and blessed it. He divided the bread, but the meal multiplied instead. He kept giving and giving the bread to the disciples, who ran from blanket to blanket, feeding family after family until everyone had eaten all they wanted with baskets of leftovers to spare.

Excuses, Excuses

Peter and the disciples did more than murmur and complain under their breath: they asked Jesus outright to send their neighbors away.

And I get it. They were physically tired. They were emotionally exhausted. They were financially strapped. They were unprepared. They were inconvenienced. And you know what? Their excuses were valid. Your own excuses may, in fact, be *fact*. You may not have enough time. You may not have the tidiest home. You may not be able to afford a gourmet meal, or even the nice kind of frozen pizza with self-rising crust. But Jesus will take whatever you offer him, and he will multiply your scraps into something you can serve to satisfy the deep needs in your neighbors.

Hospitality has more to do with sharing your life than impressing your neighbor. Hospitality can happen on the sidewalk or front porch, over store-bought cookies or a can of soda. The root of the word *hospitality* is the same as the word *hospital*, so practicing hospitality is to nurture and strengthen people so they might leave your presence feeling physically, spiritually, and emotionally fortified.

There is someone in your little corner of the world who is literally dying to hear about Jesus. This is a life-or-death situation, and our excuses don't float. There is no asterisk or exemption clause, even when we are hurting. Jesus was completely drained before he fed the five thousand. The Father did more than multiply bread and fish—he multiplied Jesus's power and strength.

Sharing something you hold dear could be the first step out of your suffering—like giving your time when you're tired, talking to a friend when you want to watch Netflix, or remembering someone's birthday when you want to forget about the rest of the world. During our most dire seasons, we can still offer someone a gentle smile.

When you're stressed, your brain is hardwired by God to crave social connections. A surprising side effect of stress is that it increases the hormone oxytocin in the brain. Known as the "love drug," oxytocin is released when you hug someone or form a social bond. It also makes you empathetic and compassionate, more willing to help others.[9] A study at the University of Buffalo concluded that people who experienced high levels of stress had a decreased risk of dying if they provided tangible assistance to friends or family. The study showed positive health outcomes as a result of helping and interacting with others—in other words, helping others helps you. Dr. Kelly McGonigal teaches, "Caring for others triggers the biology of courage and creates hope. Whether you are overwhelmed by your own stress or the suffering of others, the way to find hope is to connect, not to escape."[10]

Peter picked an interesting Greek word that's translated into English as *hospitality*, sharing your home, or having guests in your home. The compound word *philoxenos* (fil-*ox*-en-os) is a combination of these two words:[11]

- *Philos* (*fee*-los): a friend or companion. Friend of the bridegroom who asks for the hand of the bride and helps close the marriage and celebrate the wedding.[12]
- *Xenos* (*xen*-os): a foreigner or stranger, someone without knowledge.[13]

This is what we do when we show hospitality to a neighbor. We pray mindfully, love soulfully, and share cheerfully everything we have. On behalf of the Bridegroom, we take the hand of someone who doesn't know our precious friend Jesus and walk together toward God's throne. Sharing cheerfully is God's plan to reach the world with the gospel, one neighbor at a time.

A SECOND CUP

 Read Acts 17:26–27 to understand God's purpose in placing you in your neighborhood. What's happening in your neighborhood at this particular time that God might be asking you to get involved with? If your neighbors are seeking God and perhaps reaching for him, and he is "not far" from them, what are the chances they will find him hanging out over at your house? How can you let Jesus out into the neighborhood?

 Peter practiced hospitality toward his mother-in-law, as we see in Matthew 8:14, who by custom should have been living with a son instead of her daughter. It's also likely that Jesus stayed with Peter in Capernaum so often that Peter's house was considered to be Jesus's home, as we read in Mark 2:1. How do you view your home as a place of ministry? How have you been blessed by your guests, as Peter was when Jesus healed Peter's mother-in-law?

 Which one of the disciples' probable excuses do you relate to most?

> Physically tired
> Emotionally spent
> Financially strapped
> Domestically unprepared
> Overwhelmingly busy

What is one small, practical step you can take to share cheerfully with a neighbor in spite of your very real and challenging circumstances?

 Visit www.amylively.com/hospitality-quiz to discover your hospitality style, or scan this code:

Dear heavenly Father, please stretch my time and my heart so that I can share all you have given me with the people you've placed around me. Give me a cheerful heart as I walk with others toward your throne. In Jesus's name, amen.

Lesson 4

~ ❖ ~

Serve Gracefully

Read 1 Peter 4:10–11 and Acts 1–3

THE COMPANY MY HUSBAND AND I once owned built e-commerce websites, and when the pandemic started, it felt like everyone discovered the internet all at once. We were as prepared as anyone could have been—we already worked remotely, had recently expanded our team, and most importantly, we met each Monday morning to pray together. We were grateful for the influx of work and knew we were truly helping our customers, but we were plumb worn out.

So when my girlfriend offered to bring dinner, I gratefully accepted. She had no idea I'd just groaned to my husband, "I wish someone would come over and put a plate of food in front of me." (This friend happened to be Sarah's grandmother, from chapter 4!) Daily kindnesses keep us going, like a pot of soup when you're sick or a greeting card when you're lonely. Small comforts mean more than ever when big things are going wrong. Did anyone share a scarce roll of toilet paper with you, support your local business, or check in when you were shut in? Using our skills and abilities to serve one another is the secret to survival during global crises and our own personal catastrophes.

Jesus tells us to love our neighbor, care for widows, feed the needy, welcome strangers, and visit the sick, but he won't send us into the world empty-handed. He puts tools in our hands. One of the primary ways God equips us to love and serve well is through spiritual gifts. A spiritual gift is a supernatural ability given to each believer from the Holy Spirit for the purpose of fulfilling God's commands. Spiritual gifts are the secret behind Peter's next shocking survival strategy: serve gracefully.

> As each has received a gift, use it to serve one another, as good stewards of God's varied grace: whoever speaks, as one who speaks oracles of God; whoever serves, as one who serves by the strength that God supplies. (1 Peter 4:10–11)

Grace is a gift meant to be spent on others. The root word of the Greek word translated into English as *gift* (*charisma*—*khar*-is-mah) is the same as the root word of the term translated into English as *grace* (*charis*—*khar*-ece). You can regift the grace God has given you! We are managers of God's manifold, multicolored, multifaceted grace. We have set our hope fully on this grace, but along with the gift of grace comes the responsibility to steward and share it well.

I used to think my spiritual gifts were just for my personal pleasure and enjoyment. I love to teach God's Word, and some of my most fulfilling moments are spent with my Bible and notebook, coming up with new ways to explain timeless principles. It was almost an afterthought when I realized that any gift I might have for teaching was not about *me* . . . it was about *others*.

Even better, using my gift brings glory to God. Your gifts are given *to* you, but they are not *for* you. God rewards our good stewardship of his gifts with joy and fruitfulness when we use them to serve his people.

Let's unwrap the spiritual gifts Peter is talking about.

What Are Spiritual Gifts?

Peter mentions speaking and service as examples, but we find more spiritual gifts in other parts of Scripture (we'll explore Romans 12:6–8, 1 Corinthians 12:1–11, and Ephesians 4:11–12 in your Second Cup). These three lists of spiritual gifts in the New Testament use twenty Greek words altogether. Circle the ones that resonate with you and make your heart beat a little faster. Or if someone comes to mind, write their name beside their gift. In alphabetical order, the gifts are:

Administration—The ability to plan, organize, supervise, and direct people toward the accomplishment of goals. People with this gift are good at managing their time, prioritizing their work, and building a team. At church, they lead ministry teams and help run the office. If you have the urge to organize the neighborhood watch, create a neighborhood directory, or plan a block party, this may be your gift.

Apostle—Someone who leads churches with spiritual authority. Apostles may have people serving under them to help accomplish their vision for the church. During times of crisis, apostles set the attitude and direction the family or community will take toward healing.

Discernment—The ability to distinguish truth and lies. Discerning people are quick to spot a scam, are clear on doctrine, and can help point out spiritual attacks or lies of the enemy. At church, the gift of discernment can help them sense others' motives, point out when someone is trying to tear apart a team, and recognize when sermons don't line up with Scripture. During a crisis, they are alert to contradictory data and balance information from a variety of sources to determine wise strategies.

Evangelism—The fervent desire to share the good news of the gospel. Evangelists lead people to Christ on airplanes and in line at the grocery store. At church, a person with this gift might be drawn to mission trips to the far corners of the earth or right around the corner. In times of duress, evangelists check on their neighbors' hearts as well as their homes.

Exhortation—This is the person who comes running with encouragement, comfort, consolation, and counsel when anyone calls. At church, their practical, patient advice helps people become mature Christians. At home, they're the one neighbors seek for comfort for calamities from burnt dinners to overdoses.

Faith—Utter conviction about God's power and promises that is unshaken by circumstances or obstacles. If you are drawn to your church's prayer ministry and the mission field, you might have this gift. At home, nothing deters this person's hope and hard work to see salvation for their neighbors.

Giving—The ability to share material resources cheerfully and without concern for being repaid. People with this gift help with benevolence and missions and give of their time and talents as well as their funds (often anonymously). At home, they give neighbors plants from their gardens and food from their kitchens.

Healing—To be used by God to make others whole either physically, emotionally, mentally, or spiritually. Healers are a conduit for God's power. At church, you may feel the pull to regularly pray with and for others; counseling and recovery ministries are close to your heart. If your heart breaks for the suffering you see around your home, you might have this gift.

Helper—A helper gives support or assistance that frees others for ministry. You have to look hard for this person, because they happily hide in the wings and behind the scenes at church. At home, they might babysit the neighbors' children so they can go to work as well as feed the cat and water their flowers while they're on vacation.

Knowledge—An intelligence and understanding of Christianity. A person with this gift is a fact gatherer, an analyzer, an information storehouse. At church, they want to lead in-depth Bible studies; at home, they're the ones to call when their neighbors need a bit of local history or zoning laws.

Leadership—The ability to manage and motivate others to get involved. At church, leaders easily see ways to improve existing programs or develop new ones. At home, they initiate neighborhood safety watches, homeowner's associations, and holiday celebrations.

Mercy—Sensitivity and sympathy toward those who are suffering. At church, people with this gift long to embrace the lost and unlovable. Outside of church, they'll knock on a battered door to reach the battered woman inside.

Miracles—To be enabled by God with strength, power, and ability to perform supernatural feats that point to God's glory and strengthen our faith. At church, people with the gift of miracles are usually somewhere in the picture when amazing, inexplicable things happen. At home, they want to see mountains move as others' lives are transformed.

Pastor—A shepherd who finds and saves lost sheep and then loves them, patches their wounds, shares their lives, and keeps watch for predators. Pastorally gifted people can pastor a small group or ministry team; they care deeply about others' needs and growth. In the community, they're on the lookout for the lonely, the lost, and the just plain stubborn.

Prophecy—Hearing from God and speaking to people. Those with a prophetic gift have the perfect verse on the tip of their tongues to help someone at church, and at home they can apply Scripture to ordinary circumstances.

Service—The gift of knowing what needs to be done and doing it without being asked. At church, these individuals are task oriented and capable of getting more done in a day than most people do in a month. At home, they lend a hand, an ear, or a shoulder whenever neighbors need it.

Teaching—The ability to clearly explain and instruct others. At church, teachers' abilities result in understanding, application, and maturity—not just intellectual stimulation. In the community, they teach others practical skills and spiritual insight.

Tongues—The ability to speak in a language not previously learned so unbelievers can hear God's message in their own language. Tongues is directly related to . . .

Interpretation of Tongues—The ability to translate the message of someone who has spoken in tongues. At church, tongues and interpretation bring "some revelation or knowledge or prophecy or teaching" (1 Corinthians 14:6). At home, the gift of tongues could help you communicate with neighbors who speak a different language.

Wisdom—The ability to apply spiritual knowledge in practical ways in daily life. At church, people with this gift understand how to apply Scripture in context. At home, they get the desperate middle-of-the-night calls for advice.

Unwrapping Your Gifts

Peter thought he had the spiritual gift of rebuke, which, you may recall, is not on any list. Even though Peter didn't always know what to say, he didn't let that stop him from opening his mouth and inserting his foot on a regular basis. We've already seen how he tried to "heaven forbid" Christ off the cross and how a voice from heaven had to shut him up at the Transfiguration (as discussed in chapter 4).

When Peter used his own words, Jesus rebuked him and called him "Satan." When Peter spoke without thinking, God himself reprimanded him—and when Peter submitted his gifts to the Lord and was filled with the Holy Spirit, God transformed Peter from a loudmouthed loose cannon into an apostle who wrote part of the canon of Scripture. Take it from a man who heard the voice of God with his own ears: your spiritual gifts must be submitted to the Lord and used for his glory, or they will be of little use to you or anyone else.

Our favorite fisherman had an abundance of spiritual gifts that were magnificently used to glorify God. We can see many of his gifts on display in the first three chapters of Acts:

- *Apostle, administration, leadership, and knowledge* as he directed the disciples to select a replacement for Judas (Acts 1:15–20).
- *Tongues and interpretation* when the Holy Spirit rested on him and the disciples and the crowd heard the mighty works of God in their own language (Acts 2:4–11).
- *Teaching and exhortation* during the sermon at Pentecost (Acts 2:14–36).
- *Evangelism* as three thousand souls were saved (Acts 2:37–41).

- *Healing and miracles* for the lame beggar (Acts 3:1–10).
- *Faith* when announcing how the beggar was healed (Acts 3:16).

It's worth noting that people might think you're crazy when you begin using your spiritual gifts, like Peter when he was accused of being drunk when he and the others were filled with the Spirit (Acts 2:12–14). If you have the gift of discernment, others may not be able to see the truth that seems so clear to you; if you're administratively gifted, getting others to work together toward a common goal might feel like herding cats if they don't recognize your organizational gifting.

It's also worth remembering that spiritual gifts are for giving *and* receiving. Peter wrote that we should serve "by the strength that God supplies," and Lord knows, sometimes we have only a little bit of strength left. In your TEOTWAWKI times, look for others who have the gifts you need. That's what they're for! God supplies for your needs through the gifts he's given to others. Allow others to serve you and receive the blessing, fulfillment, and joy of using their gifts for God's glory in your story.

A SECOND CUP

 Read the lists of spiritual gifts in Romans 12:6–8, 1 Corinthians 12:1–11, and Ephesians 4:11–12. Which gift(s) do you think you may have? Has anyone ever complimented you on any of these gifts? Do you use any of these gifts in your workplace, at home, or in your community?

 Visit www.spiritualgiftstest.com to take a fast and free online spiritual gifts test, or ask a pastor or spiritual mentor to help you identify your gifts. Pray for God to reveal his gifts to you.

Paul said in 1 Corinthians 9:16, "Woe to me if I do not preach the gospel!" Teaching and evangelism were two of Paul's many gifts, and he felt the weight of them. What is your "Woe is me if I do not _____!"? Your favorite hobbies and the causes you support can be indicators of a gift. God also reveals our gifts through problems, compliments, career, and requests from others. What passion do you carry like a weighty gift that you feel compelled to open and use?

Dear heavenly Father, I am in awe at the bounty of gifts you have given your people! Show me the special way you've equipped me to work in your kingdom. When I am most needy, please bring people around me with the perfect mix of gifts to help me. In Jesus's name, amen.

Lesson 5

⎯ ❊ ⎯

Praise Joyfully

Read 1 Peter 4:11 and Acts 12

AFTER JESUS WAS CRUCIFIED AND resurrected but before the Holy Spirit was sent from heaven, what was a guy to do? Well, Peter went fishing—and the other disciples went, too. (I've noticed that my fishing friends never need an excuse to go fishing.) They fished all night and caught nothing. Just as day was breaking, Jesus stood on the shore, but they didn't know it was him until he loaded their nets with 153 fish! (I've also noticed that all fish enthusiasts count their catch.) You'll remember in chapter 4 when we read about their breakfast by the sea, where Jesus tenderly affirmed Peter three times to match his three betrayals. Afterward, Jesus said to Peter:

> "Truly, truly, I say to you, when you were young, you used to dress yourself and walk wherever you wanted, but when you are old, you will stretch out your hands, and another will dress you and carry you where you do not want to go." (This he said to show by what kind of death he was to glorify God.) And after saying this he said to him, "Follow me." (John 21:18–19)

When Jesus began this cryptic statement with something we usually say at the end of our prayers—"Truly, truly," or "Amen, amen"—it signaled to Peter the seriousness of this prophecy. The word Jesus chose for "dress" is *zōnnymi* (*dzone*-noo-mi), and it's only used twice in the Bible, both times regarding Peter. It would be several years before Peter would hear this word again, when he was arrested and thrown into jail at Passover—just like Jesus had been. Not wanting their prisoner to disappear, two soldiers were bound to his wrists with two chains, and two more soldiers guarded the prison door. The king planned to execute Peter to cheers of the Jewish crowd—just like they did Jesus, and also James, Peter's fishing partner and fellow apostle, who had been recently killed.

While the church urgently prayed, Peter easily slept. (Peter still had no problem sleeping while others prayed.) His wife may have led the charge; she was surely with the large crowd huddled together making intercession to God to spare Peter's life. If you've pleaded for the life of your spouse, your child, your parent, or someone you love, then you know the intensity of her prayers. You would do anything to give them peace or take their place.

Peter was not being inattentive to "earnest and disciplined prayers" as he slept; he was displaying the gentle and quiet spirit that is so precious to God (1 Peter 3:4). He didn't awaken until his cell filled with light and an angel elbowed him in the side, saying:

> "Get up quickly." And the chains fell off his hands. And the angel said to him, "Dress yourself and put on your sandals." And he did so. And he said to him, "Wrap your cloak around you and follow me." (Acts 12:7–8)

"The very fact that, on the night before what he knows will be his execution, he can sleep so soundly that it requires a sound angelic thump on the side to waken him, reveals the profound courage Jesus had instilled in his heart and mind," said songwriter and author Michael Card.[14] Like rousing a sleepy teenager to go to church, the angel had to coach Peter to dress himself—and I wonder if Peter's mind instantly flew back to Jesus's parting words during their breakfast by the sea about someone dressing him and taking him where he didn't want to go. Was this the end?

This was not the end, at least not yet. Peter safely returned to his church, and the word of God increased and multiplied along with the number of souls that were added to it.

Peter likely wouldn't have forgotten that word, and he doesn't want you to forget, either. The root word Jesus used for *dress* is the same word Peter used for "prepare your minds for action"—get dressed for battle, gird up the loins of your mind, put on your big girl pants—and set your hope fully on Jesus:

> Therefore, *preparing your minds for action*, and being sober-minded, set your hope fully on the grace that will be brought to you at the revelation of Jesus Christ. (1 Peter 1:13)

When the grace of Jesus Christ is revealed, our only response is praise. Even when we're suffering? Especially then! In every single chapter, Peter's encouragement to praise God is *always* accompanied by a pain point:

1 Peter	Pain	Praise
1:6	though now for a little while, if necessary, you have been grieved by various trials	in this you rejoice
1:7	the tested genuineness of your faith—more precious than gold that perishes though it is tested by fire	may be found to result in praise and glory and honor at the revelation of Jesus Christ

1:8	though you do not now see him	you believe in him and rejoice with joy that is inexpressible and filled with glory
1:11	the sufferings of Christ	the subsequent glories
2:9–10	once you were not a people…once you had not received mercy	you are a chosen race, a royal priesthood, a holy nation, a people for his own possession, that you may proclaim the excellencies of him who called you out of darkness into his marvelous light
2:12	when they speak against you as evildoers	they may see your good deeds and glorify God on the day of visitation
3:14–15	if you should suffer for righteousness's sake	you will be blessed. Have no fear of them, nor be troubled, but in your hearts honor Christ the Lord as holy
4:13	rejoice insofar as you share Christ's sufferings	that you may also rejoice and be glad when his glory is revealed
4:16	if anyone suffers as a Christian	let him not be ashamed, but let him glorify God in that name
5:10–11	after you have suffered a little while	the God of all grace, who has called you to his eternal glory in Christ, will himself restore, confirm, strengthen, and establish you. To him be the dominion forever and ever. Amen.

This is Peter's final strategy for surviving the end of the world as you know it: praise joyfully. He wrapped up this battle plan with a worshipful shout:

In order that in everything God may be glorified through Jesus Christ. To him belong glory and dominion forever and ever. Amen. (1 Peter 4:11)

Peter can't stop praising God; he had to say it again!

To him be the dominion forever and ever. Amen. (1 Peter 5:11)

Jesus's TEOTWAWKI Strategy

Where did Peter get this plan? From Jesus, of course. Go back with me to the Last Supper, where we already spent some time in chapter 4. Jesus employed each of these strategies that night, which you can explore in your Second Cup:

- He *prayed mindfully* in Gethsemane and in his High Priestly Prayer.
- He *loved soulfully* right to the end.
- He *shared cheerfully* the bread and wine of the Passover meal.
- He *served gracefully* when he washed the disciples' feet.
- He *praised joyfully* by singing a hymn after the meal.

And when they had sung a hymn, they went out to the Mount of Olives. (Matthew 26:30)

Wouldn't you love to hear the voice of Jesus singing? While we don't know the tune, we can be certain that the hymn was from Psalm 118. The group of psalms from chapters 113–118 are called the Hallel (haw-*lail*), which means praise. It's the root of the word *hallelujah*, which means "praise the LORD." The Hallel is a collection of praises for the Lord's provision, protection, and power, his steadfast love and faithfulness, his trustworthy help, and eternal salvation. The last Hallel, Psalm 118, was traditionally sung as the Passover meal ended.

This means that on the day Jesus was betrayed, denied, accused, mocked, beaten, abandoned, rejected, scorned, and spit upon, just before he was tortured, crucified, and buried, it is likely that he sang the words of Psalm 118, which include this verse:

This is the day that the LORD has made; let us rejoice and be glad in it. (Psalm 118:24)

Sit with that a minute. This is the single day that defines suffering more than any other. And it's a day of rejoicing, even gladness. Jesus was joyful to gaze upon his cross. Assured that his prayer would not fail and his Father would be glorified, he was glad. Knowing that his suffering on one day impacted every day for everyone forevermore, Jesus rejoiced.

Peter said "in *everything* God may be glorified through Jesus Christ"—*every* good thing, *every* hard thing, *every* uncertain thing, *every* unbearable thing. Every. Thing.

God is never so near as when we are brokenhearted and beat down. He is faithful and true, ready to give grace and mercy. He stands ready to receive our praise—"Holy! Holy! Holy!"—and the angels join our chorus. He is never so worthy of our praise as when he walks with us through our darkest days, our toughest trials, our life-altering, earth-shaking, what-in-the-world-will-I-do moments.

When you're in the middle of a trial, you might be tempted to pick up the phone, start making some calls, manipulate the outcome, intervene, control, plead, beg, and bribe—or maybe that's just me. When we are suffering, these strategies Peter learned from Jesus align with Scripture and lead to spiritual success:

- *Pray mindfully* with your mind fully focused on God and your hope fully set on his grace. Enter your Gethsemane with lament, anguish, and confusion, and rise with conviction, compassion, and power when your heart's prayer is to glorify God.

- *Love soulfully* with an unconditional, unceasing, unwavering, and unrelenting love. Undeserved love, uncomfortable love, the kind of love that stretches your heart to the breaking point. This kind of love will cost you something. It did Christ.
- *Share cheerfully* and take part in God's plan to reach the world with the gospel, one neighbor at a time.
- *Serve gracefully* by using the spiritual gifts given to you from God for others and receiving the gifts he's given to others for you.
- *Praise joyfully* and transform your suffering into worship. Remembering God's goodness changes anxiety into adoration. Turmoil, confusion, despair, and worry about personal circumstances fade into the background as we turn our eyes upon Jesus, who suffered once for all and rose again as our living hope.

The contrast between Peter's impulsive old self and his Spirit-filled new self is obvious. The man who fell asleep while praying was eventually able to urge us to *pray mindfully*. He was changed from a quarrelsome, prideful, and prejudiced man into a peaceful and accepting apostle as he learned to *love soulfully*. Before he could encourage us to *share cheerfully*, he wanted to send his neighbors away to fend for themselves. God took a strong-willed, outspoken guy and transformed him into a humble man who used his gifts to *serve gracefully*. We follow his example as we *praise joyfully* during our perplexing trials.

Peter's letters would have been shredded had he not shown the same courage, faith, and worship that he exhorted the "elect exiles" to display—they would have called out his hypocrisy in a heartbeat. But the crowd of witnesses saw how Peter's faith survived his head-on collision with real life. According to historians, they gathered near the shadow of a massive obelisk in the center of the Circus of Nero in ancient Rome and watched as Peter stretched out his hands and was led where he did not want to go.[15] Today, we can remember Peter's faithfulness to his risen Savior at St. Peter's Basilica in Vatican City, erected over the spot where he is believed to have been martyred.

Jesus prayed for Peter that his faith would not fail, and Peter stood fast to the end. Jesus's last words to Peter were the same as his first words—"Follow me" (Mark 1:17 and John 21:19). Knowing his faith in Christ would ultimately lead to his own death but would bring glory to God, Peter did follow Jesus, all the way to his own upside-down cross, his wife by his side, as he comforts and encourages her, "O thou, remember the Lord!"

A SECOND CUP

 How did Jesus describe the outcome of Peter's death in John 21:19? Read Hebrews 12:2. How did watching Jesus die affect Peter's attitude toward his own death? What do you think was on Peter's mind as someone dressed him and led him where he did not want to go—and his wife, too? How should their experiences and testimony impact our attitude toward suffering, and even death?

 For an extreme example of what happens when we don't praise joyfully, read Acts 12:21–23 for the fate of the king who ordered Peter's imprisonment. What is God's reaction when his glory is stolen? Compare this to Psalm 115:1, which is part of the Hallel that Jesus may have sung at the last Passover. According to this verse, why is God worthy of our praise? How have you seen these qualities of God in your own life?

Read Psalm 118. Knowing Jesus likely sang this on the night he was betrayed, which verses do you think specifically encouraged him? Bookmark this psalm to read when you are afraid or are facing a trial.

Peter developed this survival plan by observing Jesus:

- He *prayed mindfully* in Gethsemane and in his High Priestly Prayer (John 17).
- He *loved soulfully* right to the end (John 13:1).
- He *shared cheerfully* the Passover meal (Matthew 26:26–29).
- He *served gracefully* when he washed the disciples' feet (John 13:3–5).
- He *praised joyfully* by singing traditional hymns after the meal (Matthew 26:30).

Write in your journal about a specific way you will apply Jesus's strategy to your own TEOTWAWKI moment.

Visit www.amylively.com/playlist to listen to free hope-filled worship music or scan this code:

Read 1 Peter 1–5 in your Bible and mark each passage about a reaction we can control in crisis, no matter what craziness is going on around us:

Dear heavenly Father, you have sent your Son before me to show me how to suffer gloriously. In my deepest pain, I want to honor you. Please save me, and give me success in these strategies. In Jesus's name, amen.

CHAPTER 6

YOUR STORY FOR GOD'S GLORY

1 Peter 5

CAN YOU DO ME A favor? Next time I write a book, remind me to pick something easy like *How to Tell Jokes that Make Kids Laugh* or *Raising Goldfish for Dummies*. Suffering is a hard topic, and I felt overwhelmed as I immersed myself in others' stories and juggled my own new normal.

Then I got a frightening middle-of-the-night text when friends were badly injured in a motorcycle accident. *Hopefully, they'll be okay . . .*

And I had a long conversation with someone I love very much on the brink of a very bad decision. *Hopefully, he'll make a wise choice . . .*

My prayer list was packed with urgent needs like the suicide of a local student, a deadly house fire, and friends with looming money problems, difficult marriages, unruly kids, and lonely empty nests. *Hopefully, I can help . . .*

There were mind-numbing videos on my news feed, contention and dissension on every side over every issue. *Hopefully, our world will heal . . .*

To top it off, I was stressed about a complex project with a looming deadline and a to-do list bigger than my brain. *Hopefully, I'll get it all done . . .*

This load of sorrow and sadness seemed as large and heavy as the mountains surrounding my home. I needed to refill my cup of hope, and fast! Then I remembered hearing something about setting my hope fully on the grace given when Christ is revealed, and the voice in my head sounded strangely like my own.

"Hope fully" is a good idea, but does it work?

The fifth and final chapter of 1 Peter assures us that it does! Hope in Christ is a successful survival strategy for suffering. It's also a compelling story for the crowd of witness who is watching to see if we survive when our faith in Christ has a head-on collision with real-life problems.

This is the theme of 1 Peter 5. When you see verses about the impact our testimony makes in the lives of others, draw a circle with smaller circles inside, like the ripples of a pebble tossed into a pond.

Let's look back over what Peter has taught us in 1 Peter 1–4 as we come to his fifth, farewell chapter. We'll see how our stories are bigger than ourselves with an ending that's better than we could have ever imagined. Our four special guests will be joined by one more woman I've been wanting to hear from for a long time, and her story will amaze you!

 Scan this code or visit www.amylively.com/cup-of-hope /#chapter6 to access online resources and read the Scripture passages online.

A Look Back

Read 1 Peter 5

Turning the pages of 1 Peter in my Bible, I saw symbols I had drawn that reminded me of the themes Peter returned to again and again. With a litany of urgent requests stirring my heart, I looked back at the four incredible women who so vulnerably and bravely shared their suffering with us. Chapter by chapter, their stories align perfectly with the themes of Peter's letter, and Peter's final chapter wraps each story with a beautiful bow.

Heaven and the Here and Now: 1 Peter 1

I reminded myself of Michelle's beautiful smile through her sorrowful tears. The last time I saw her husband, my dear friend Joe, his body had faded like the flower described in 1 Peter 1:24. I saw firsthand how Joe took full advantage of the attention he received during his suffering to praise God publicly and ask people pointed questions about their own faith. Joe and Michelle both placed their hope fully in Peter's promise:

> Humble yourselves, therefore, under the mighty hand of God so that at the proper time he may exalt you. (1 Peter 5:6)

Sometimes, the "proper time" happens here on earth, so until the Lord says otherwise, I will beg for health for those who are sick and ailing. God cares so much about the here and now. It's a difficult yet magnificent concept to grasp that if we are not healed here, in the way we expect in the time we desire, we are completely healed in heaven, our salvation secure for all eternity. Michelle's cup of hope, once filled with visions of growing old with her husband, now sparkles with the champagne of an eternal perspective.

I synchronized my prayers with God's eternal clock to gain an eternal perspective of the immediate needs on my heart. I thanked God for the promise Peter recorded that this suffering will not last forever. I prayed for God to use each circumstance—even the painful ones—to turn hearts toward him. I asked for patience and grace as our world unraveled. I prayed that my daily interactions would open doors to holy conversations with lasting implications long after tasks and projects were complete.

Just like Jesus: 1 Peter 2

I remembered Kelly's TEOTWAWKI moment in the principal's office when she learned her son had been hit by a Jeep while riding his bike home from the gym. She packed a suitcase in fifteen minutes and didn't return home for seven months as she accompanied Josh to hospitals across the country. Josh, whose life verse is 1 Peter 2:17, was perfectly prepared before the accident for the long recovery from his traumatic brain injury. In college, he told a classmate he memorized Scripture in case there ever came a time he couldn't read his Bible. A previous injury during naval training paved the way for veteran's benefits to cover his care. Kelly sets her hope fully on God's grace, as she patiently walks the path God has chosen for her, eagerly anticipating the day Josh will walk it with her. Kelly's cup of hope was never filled with the Hollywood ending she once imagined, but it now overflows with gratitude and a deep, abiding trust in God.

Although I went to the hospital to minister to their family, they have been the ones to minister to me. They taught me that when God allows us to suffer, he supplies all our needs. He doesn't expect us to carry these heavy burdens without his help. Just like he did for Jesus, he sustains us until he reveals the happy ending he's already written to our story:

Casting all your anxieties on him, because he cares for you. (1 Peter 5:7)

Kelly's story reminded me that my Father chose me for such a time as this. He assessed my strengths and considered my weaknesses, my talents and skills, my personality, my experiences, my neighbors and community. Knowing this, knowing me, he said, "Her. I choose her. She is exactly who I need for such a time as this. She is precious. She's perfect, and she's mine."

How to Handle an Unholy Mess: 1 Peter 3

I looked at my faded wedding pictures and saw a much younger Jennifer standing beside me, eight months pregnant in a billowing bridesmaid's gown. When we were in one another's weddings we couldn't have imagined her painful divorce. Her only goal was to hold her head high, no matter what happened. Jennifer followed Peter's instruction to wives in 1 Peter 3 and watched her family follow Jesus in her footsteps in an untimely answer to her prayers. Her holy conduct during an unholy mess was a powerful example to all who watched it unfold.

Lead them by your own good example. (1 Peter 5:3 NLT)

Jennifer left her cup of hope in the kitchen sink where her world imploded. Her honorable behavior honored God, and she received a new cup free of cracks and stains.

I asked myself, what would people know about me by my conduct in each of these situations where I was burdened—and would my behavior lead them to praise Jesus? Did I offer practical assistance like a meal or help around the house—or did I put the burden on them to "call me if you need anything"? Was I really sending the prayers I had promised? I asked one simple question to figure out how to handle each challenging situation: "What's the holy thing to do?"

Before and After: 1 Peter 4

I looked across the valley from my home and could see the chimney of Sarah's grandparents' home. God answered Sarah's grandmother's prayers and rescued Sarah from a life of addiction, abuse, alcoholism, and anger. What Satan meant for evil in her life, God used for good. Only God himself can move a person from such pain to promise, but Sarah did the hard work of conforming her will to God's ways as we read in the fourth chapter of 1 Peter. The poison that once infused her cup was rinsed clean, and her cup was newly filled up with hope and promise. Sarah endured to the end, and she'll be justly rewarded:

> And when the chief Shepherd appears, you will receive the unfading crown of glory. (1 Peter 5:4)

Sarah's beautiful "Before and After" story encouraged me to crucify my own desires for these situations and surrender my hopes and dreams along with my fears and worries into God's capable, caring hands.

How to Survive the End of the World: 1 Peter 4:7–11

Whew. That was close! I could feel the dark cloud of despair closing in on me, but my perspective changed as these women's stories reframed my problems through the lens of 1 Peter. They helped me recall Peter's five spiritual strategies that I can control when my world comes crashing down.

I began to *pray mindfully* and asked, "Father, glorify your name!" instead of, "Give me what I want!"

I thought of ways to *love soulfully* and express God's lovingkindness to each hurting heart.

I searched for any resource I could *share cheerfully* to ease their burdens.

Using my blend of spiritual gifts, I sought ways to *serve gracefully.*

Then I paused to *praise joyfully* for what God had already done and was going to do in each person's life and waited expectantly for him to work.

One by one, each friend poured generously into my dry, empty cup until it brimmed fully with hope.

Your Story for God's Glory: 1 Peter 5

Early in Jesus's ministry, he lived in the region of Galilee in the village of Capernaum, by the sea—probably in Peter's home along with Peter's wife and mother-in-law.[1] Seven hundred years before Christ, God announced his plan to put him in Peter's neighborhood when the prophet Isaiah said this about the coming Messiah:

> The way of the sea, beyond the Jordan, Galilee of the Gentiles— the people dwelling in darkness have seen a great light, and for those dwelling in the region and shadow of death, on them a light has dawned. (Matthew 4:15–16)

Great crowds of people followed Jesus as he preached the gospel of the kingdom and healed disease and affliction. Peter and his wife and mother-in-law, along with Mary, the mother of Jesus, and the other disciples and their families, were all probably listening when Jesus preached a famous sermon on a mount in Galilee. All eyes were on Jesus as he said:

> "You are the light of the world. A city set on a hill cannot be hidden. Nor do people light a lamp and put it under a basket, but on a stand, and it gives light to all in the house. In the same way, let your light shine before others, so that they may see your good works and give glory to your Father who is in heaven." (Mathew 5:14–16)

No one else can shine quite like you do. Your lantern is cracked and dented by the hammer of hardship so that the light of God's glory casts a unique glow through your story.

Letting our light shine before others is the endgame of suffering. In the end, it's not about the lamp—it's about the Light.

Michelle, Kelly, Jennifer, and Sarah shared their stories for God's glory . . . but there's one more story that needs to be told.

Yours.

A SECOND CUP

 Which woman's story resonated most with you, and why? If you send them a note of encouragement at www.amy lively.com/contact (or scan this code for quick access), I will make sure they receive it!

 On a scale of 1–5, rate your eagerness to share your story:

1	2	3	4	5
Where's the door? I'm outta here!	What story? I'm too ordinary.	I'll pray about it for a few years.	I'll share with a close friend.	Gimme the micro- phone!

 Read 1 Peter in your Bible, and mark any verse about the compelling nature of our testimony with circles within a circle, like the ripple of a stone thrown in a pond.

Dear heavenly Father, thank you for encouraging me with the stories in Scripture and the stories taking place right on my street. If you want to speak to others through my own experience, I am willing to be used for your glory. In Jesus's name, amen.

Lesson 2

— ❋ —

How to Share Your Story

Read 1 Peter 3:15, 2 Corinthians 1:8–9, and Romans 12:15

SHARING YOUR STORY MIGHT FEEL as nerve-racking as public speaking before a large crowd—naked. God may ask you to do that someday (with clothes on, of course), but mostly our stories are shared on park benches or at kitchen tables, intimate settings where we can look into someone's weary eyes and wipe away one another's tears. Peter reminds us that people are watching and desperately waiting to hear about the cup of hope they see you carrying:

> In your hearts honor Christ the Lord as holy, always being prepared to make a defense to anyone who asks you for a reason for the hope that is in you; yet do it with gentleness and respect. (1 Peter 3:15)

The Greek word for *defense* is *apologia* (ap-ol-og-*ee*-ah), and it means a reasoned statement or argument. It's where the term *apologetics* comes from, which means defending one's faith. But your story isn't a debate or a contest of ideas; it's not an argument to be won with cold, hard facts. Stories are told in vivid color! No one can dispute your personal experience of walking with Christ and how he refilled your cup of hope when you were parched and weary. Your personal testimony is an interesting, intriguing, nonthreatening, and relevant way to open a conversation about Christ. This is what Peter and his friend and fellow disciple John did:

> We cannot stop telling about everything we have seen and heard. (Acts 4:20 NLT)

When you tell what you have seen and heard, sharing your faith becomes natural and practical. There's nothing to memorize, because you lived every excruciating detail! You were there, you know it best—and God will use your style and personality to tell your tale perfectly. God will use your story as his megaphone to speak into someone else's life.

You don't have to broadcast your whole life history in one sitting—you can share a single episode that happened at the grocery store or one challenging scene at work. Here are four steps to spiritual storytelling that will shine your story into a dark world.

1. Recognize

Recognize that God is producing and directing your story. The people in the Bible didn't know they were in the Bible; they were just living their lives, doing their jobs, raising their kids. The little spaces between chapters were sometimes agonizingly long times in reality. They had no idea that someone was going to write down their story so that people would read about their mistakes or their victories for the next few thousand years.

Spiritual story lines are being written as you respond and react to situations. People and problems that interrupt your day aren't sidelines; they're headlines, and each interaction has the potential to be a major plot twist for any one of the characters. Pause and ask the

Lord, "What are you up to here? What role do you want me to play in this story?" Your neighbors and children and family are watching your story unfold—maybe with popcorn!

2. Recall

Next, recall specific incidents of God's grace. The amazing coincidences and last-minute miracles you don't think you'll ever forget will all become a fog after a few years. The big stories are obvious and easy to remember, even if they're difficult to put into words. Keep your eyes open to smaller revelations, too, little glimpses of God's goodness. Spotting the everyday miracles in our mundane moments inspires hope in us and others.

Yes, you should share your incriminating blunders—if Peter can air his dirty laundry, then so can you—but not the names or deeds of other participants. At the end of this book is a template you can use to rehearse your story, where you'll decide what to leave in and what to leave out to protect the innocent (and the guilty).

3. Reapply

Then, reapply your story to broader scenarios. You can turn the sequence of events and the actual, factual details of your story into a living, breathing narrative that will be useful in other circumstances. The word *narrative* is from the Latin verb that means "to know." Don't you really want "to know" what God was up to when all this was happening? An incident about money may have a message about trust, or an argument over dinner may hold a lesson in kindness.

Okay, I *am* speaking from personal experience—my husband and I had our first big fight as a newly married couple about how to cook green beans, and we still disagree. Find the larger story so that when your specific circumstances change, you'll still remember a general principle you can use over and over again. For example, you can show kindness to your husband by doing simple things that please him, like cooking green beans until they're a mushy lump instead of fresh and crisp the way God meant for vegetables to be eaten.

4. Release

When it's time to release your story, don't spew it all over an unsuspecting friend. First give it a little thought and a lot of prayer. There's a rubric at the end of the book as well as an online resource that will help you record pertinent details you will want to include—or omit—depending on the situation. Consider what to leave in, what to leave out, when to shut up, and when to speak up.

What to Leave In

- *Leave in the facts.* To make sure you correctly remember your own story, you can take notes or keep a journal, look at your calendar or your photos, or check your social media memories. It's amazing what we forget! After a while, I can't remember what year something happened, let alone God's split-second timing. Factual details in a story make it credible. Archaeologists have unearthed thousands of artifacts that confirm biblical dates, places, rulers, wars, or people, adding to the Bible's trustworthiness and reliability.

- *Leave in the feelings.* Emotions are the difference between a story and a lecture. It may be harder for you to tell a story that evokes a lot of feeling, but it's easier for your listener to remember. Emotion makes your story stick. Jesus in Gethsemane was anguished and distraught to the point of sweating blood. On the cross he cried out that he felt abandoned, rejected, and alone. Peter wept bitterly when he betrayed Jesus. The lower we go in the middle of our stories, the higher the praise goes at the end.

- *Leave in the ugly.* Leave in the embarrassing blunders and bloopers, the smack-your-head, "What was I thinking?" moments.

Don't sugarcoat your testimony to make it sweeter to swallow. The ugly parts are where people make a connection, where they identify . . . because we're all just a little messed up, aren't we? The awkward parts make your story relatable. You cannot read an uglier book than our own Bible, full of murderers, liars, adulterers, and thieves—and those are the good guys!

What to Leave Out

- *Leave out the innocent.* Don't share personal, embarrassing, or confidential details about someone else. Don't say anything you wouldn't say in front of them, and always assume your words will come back to them. Protect others' privacy unless you have permission to share their stories.
- *Leave out the guilty.* There's an antagonist in every story. If they're still living and still part of your world, leave room for redemption and the possibility of reconciliation. Ask yourself if what you're sharing would be helpful or harmful, and avoid mother-in-law syndrome (when your mother can't forgive your spouse because of all the negative things you've said about them).
- *Leave out gory details.* Leave out your bodily functions, sex life, and surgical procedures. Keep it dinner-table clean so people can focus on the story without getting sick. I want to know the depth of your pain, but when you see your listener start to shudder, it's time to stop. Unless someone is a nurse, you don't need to tell each test result or medicine dosage—and no one ever needs to see your kidney stone.
- *Leave out lewdness.* Don't let your story lead someone into temptation. Don't glorify your sin, and don't make it funny. Don't provide an instruction manual on how to do it. Give just enough information so that someone understands what you're talking about but can't picture it in vivid detail.

When to Shut Up

- *Shut up when you're still bleeding.* If you're still bleeding with anger, resentment, malice, or bitterness, you may not be ready to tell your story in a way that will bless somebody else. Sometimes we need to wait until our wounds have had time to turn to scars before releasing our stories. The painful memories and emotions associated with your scar may never go away, but any trace of bitterness, resentfulness, or unforgiveness communicates the wrong message and leaves the listener with the wrong conclusion. I'm not saying we must be silent until we're completely healed, but that we must examine our heart before releasing our hurt.

- *Shut up when they're still crying.* Make sure your story is appropriate to your audience's circumstances and state of mind. If you have a similar story to theirs and you've already had a happy ending, spend a good bit of time empathizing with the other person before you reveal the climactic ending. Compassionately enter into their story by sharing in their pain, not your progress.

When to Speak Up

- *Speak up when you can share the gospel.* Our stories don't have the weight of Scripture, but they are a way to Scripture. As British evangelist Rodney Smith said, "There are five Gospels: Matthew, Mark, Luke, John, and the Christian. Most people will never read the first four."[2] Memorize a simple gospel message such as, "For the wages of sin is death, but the free gift of God is eternal life in Christ Jesus our Lord" (Romans 6:23), and practice explaining what it means.

- *Speak up when you can speak life.* Speak up when you can speak hope into someone's helplessness. You may have a story that is important and deep and tragic and emotional. If it was a big deal in your home, it could be a big deal in your neighbor's. We rob others of comfort when we hoard our story.

Our Lord literally wrote a book of individual people's stories. Re-telling our story for God's glory is how suffering becomes worship and our hardships become harbingers of God's grace for others.

A SECOND CUP

 Use the chart in the appendix or visit www.amylively.com /my-story for an interactive storytelling template you can customize, save, and print. While you're there, you can sign up for a free five-day devotional about sharing your story based on 1 Peter 3:15. Scan this code for quick access:

 Identify a time in your life when you know the Lord was working in your heart—it may have been a problem or dilemma, a change, a time of suffering, or a conflict. It may be a whole season, or perhaps it's only one scene. You probably already have a title for this story in your head, like "That Time I Moved to Colorado" or "The Flat Tire."

 Jot down the details of this episode—timelines, timely revelations, the people involved, what was happening, where you were, when the events took place, what else was happening in the world and in your life.

 What did God teach you through your own story? How has that lesson lingered or been reapplied to other scenarios? Which Scriptures were most meaningful to you at that time?

 What facts should you include when you release your story? What were you feeling at the time? What details or names should be purposely omitted as you tell your story?

Dear heavenly Father, open my ears to opportunities to share my story, and train me to tell it well. You comforted me so that I can comfort others. Please give me confidence and grace as I remember all you've done in my life. In Jesus's name, amen.

Lesson 3

Glory Revealed

Read 1 Peter 5:8–11

FROM GENESIS 1 TO REVELATION 21, God's glory is revealed on every page of your Bible. Peter can't stop talking about God's glory. Nearly 10 percent of the verses in 1 Peter are about the *doxa* (*dox*-ah), or glory, of God—his splendor and brilliance, his honor and praise, his light and loveliness. Peter began the final chapter in his short letter to the early church with this reminder:

> I, too, will share in his glory when he is revealed to the whole world. (1 Peter 5:1 NLT)

The word Peter used for "revealed" is *apokalyptō* (ap-ok-al-*oop*-tow). This root word of *apocalypse* is more than a mysterious, far-off, end-time event; it's the full disclosure of the glory of God and the realization of hope right here, today, for you, for real. Someday every eye in the sky will see the second coming of the Lord Jesus Christ. Until then, God's glory is revealed in your own personal apocalypses.

It is hard to explain how God's glory breaks through our most difficult dilemmas, our TEOTWAWKI moments, our seasons of uncertainty, and our days of despair. Oh, but he does—he can, and he most definitely will. As we hope fully just in Jesus, God reveals his magnificence and majesty, his glory and goodness—and our only response is to fall flat on our face in worship.

First to You

You'll be the first to see God's glory in your own story. Even as you lie face down weeping on the floor, you'll know he's near. Your Bible will fall open to a random passage that heals your heart. A friend will call at just the right moment with the perfect advice. Podcasts, songs, and memes will speak directly to your need. And don't even get me started on Sunday sermons; they'll be so spot-on you'll think the preacher is reading your journal. The weight of the world on your shoulders will be replaced by the weighty presence of the Holy Spirit himself:

> If you are insulted for the name of Christ, you are blessed, because the Spirit of glory and of God rests upon you. (1 Peter 4:14)

Rest is a picture of God's Spirit hugging you tight, replacing your tossing and turning with a sense of quiet, calm, and patient expectation. This pause refreshes your mind and renews your strength. The Spirit of glory will pick you gently off the ground and stand you on your own two feet. The Spirit of God will wipe your tears.

Now remember, we're not talking about suffering for being thoughtless or careless—that's another matter entirely. This is about suffering for being a Christian. When you dare to claim the blood of Christ as forgiveness for your sins, you stir a hornet's nest in the spiritual realm and sometimes even in your own home. And that kind of spiritual persecution? It moves the heavens.

Peter suffered plenty at his own hand. His own brash behavior and his bitter betrayals caused him incredible humiliation and grief. One of the ways the Bible proves it's reliable and true is the downright embarrassing stories it tells of its greatest heroes. You can't make this stuff up!

I've brought so much of my own suffering upon myself, like Peter did, when I've made my own bad decisions and faced the consequences. But as many times as Peter failed to follow his own advice, his imperfect life (and his upside-down death) glorified God. When the Spirit of glory and of God rested on him, Peter aligned his stumbling steps to the footprints of his friend and Savior, Jesus Christ. Peter was not disqualified by his mistakes or defined by his scars, and neither are you. Even life's awkward and uncomfortable scenes can be filtered through God's grace to show his glory and his power.

A crowd of bystanders is watching to see if you'll emerge from the head-on collision of your Christian faith and real-life crisis. They heard the squealing brakes and saw the impact, and they're anxiously peering into the smoke to see if you survived the crash.

You'll walk away from this wreck with bandages and scars—and a story.

Then to Others

The gawking crowd has also been wrecked by suffering. They understand your pain; they feel it in their souls, too. They recognize injustice; they have been victims, too. They know what persecution is; they may have even been on the giving end of it.

Abused? *Been there.*
Betrayed? *Done that.*
Confused? *Every day.*
Anxious? *Always.*

Then there's you.
It could be that you've been through the same suffering, but there's

something special about you. A neighbor once told me, "I call myself a Christian, but I don't really do anything religious. I own a Bible, but I've never read it. For me to even open a Bible would be a big deal. But I see people who have faith go through things like I've gone through—and even worse—and they seem to have a hope that I don't have. I know I can get it, but I don't know how. I don't even know where to start." Well, she started right there in my living room as I filled her cup with the hope that I have.

This is how God answers the prayer that never fails, "Father, glorify your name." When God reveals his glory to you, you get to pour it back to the world. When the Spirit of glory gives you power and grace to forgive the unforgiveable, love the unlovable, and do the impossible, it does not go unnoticed.

Your history is his story. Your story *compels* others first to wonder, then to worship.

Suffering is universal, but your story is unique, and someone in the world needs to hear it:

Resist him [the devil], firm in your faith, knowing that the same kinds of suffering are being experienced by your brotherhood throughout the world. (1 Peter 5:9)

There had never before been a global experience like we all shared with COVID-19. Yes, there have been pandemics, but not in the age of international travel, interwoven economies, and incessant, instant information. At breakneck speed, hundreds of millions of people on every continent linked their germy hands, coming into close enough proximity to one another to spread a microscopic molecule from person to person to person.

Do you realize what this means for the gospel? What if we spread the life-giving word of hope instead of a deadly disease? The impact of your story for God's glory can travel farther, faster than ever before!

Jesus knew his *why*. He understood the point of his pain:

> For Christ also suffered once for sins, the righteous for the
> unrighteous, that he might bring us to God. (1 Peter 3:18)

God's greater purpose in Christ's suffering was to gather us to his
pierced side, bring us peace through his punishment, and heal us with
his wounds. Our purpose in suffering is the same as Christ's: to reveal
God's grace and glory and to gather others. God reveals his glory *to* you,
then *through* you. Your hallelujahs during hardship and faith refined by
fire are used to comfort others in crisis and *compel* them toward the cross.

And in the Heavenly Places

There's more going on in your story than you may realize. Your story
has layers and depth, meaning and significance far greater than meets
the human eye. But you've already sensed that, haven't you? You've
smelled the evil lurking behind a simple insult and have fought an
enemy much fiercer than any cancer diagnosis. First, the bad news: the
battle is real.

> Be sober-minded; be watchful. Your adversary the devil
> prowls around like a roaring lion, seeking someone to devour.
> (1 Peter 5:8)

Satan demanded permission to have at Peter, to devour him, sift
him and shake him, rattle and agitate him. This diabolic scheme still
plays out every single day in our own lives. There's more bad news
for those who don't have the hope of Jesus Christ: hell is real, too.
This isn't a threat or condemnation, it's a statement of fact according
to Scripture (Matthew 10:28). This reality creates urgency to share the
word that was preached to you in your darkest hour, when you needed
it most, and helps you swallow that lump in your throat the next time

the Holy Spirit gives you a hard elbow in the side and urges you to share your hope with someone whose cup is empty.

To us, Peter says (and who knew this better than Peter?) we should be sober-minded, clearheaded, and bright-eyed for this battle.

> Resist him, firm in your faith. . . . And after you have suffered a little while, the God of all grace, who has called you to his eternal glory in Christ, will himself restore, confirm, strengthen, and establish you. To him be the dominion forever and ever. Amen. (1 Peter 5:9–11)

When you're under attack, Jesus leaps to his feet to intercede for you. When you glorify God during your heartache, angels give high fives. When you overcome the enemy, cherubim cheer. The Holy Spirit carries your frantic prayers to heaven where they become a fragrant offering before the Father's throne. When your love stamps out hatred, angels sing. When you sing, heaven shakes! When you surrender your suffering, heaven's army fights the battle for you.

The scene in your family room or your hospital room, the courtroom or the classroom, has a host of witnesses unseen to you. Of course, your children are watching, your spouse or family are taking notes, your neighbors overhear—and there are also rulers and authorities in the heavenly places who are waiting to see how your story ends.

What you believe about the end of your story determines how you will live in the middle. Walk worthy, dear one. Live a story worth telling, then tell it well.

A SECOND CUP

 Have you felt closer to God in your seasons of distress or in times of blessing? How have you experienced the

Spirit of glory resting on you during suffering (1 Peter 4:14)? Do you ever miss those intimate days with him?

 When has your own bad behavior brought about your suffering? How did God show grace to you during that season? How did he redeem your mistakes?

 Who has shared their story with you at the perfect moment, with the perfect message? What were you going through at the time? How did their sympathy and compassion bless you? What would it feel like to know that your story could similarly impact another person who is hurting?

 Read Ephesians 3:7–13 and Ephesians 6:12. How does it change your perspective to know that your personal struggles are being observed in the spiritual realm? When have you sensed angels watching over you or demons antagonizing you?

Dear heavenly Father, I am part of a much bigger story than I realized. Please use my tests and trials to draw me close to you, then use my story to draw others in. May my walk be a witness to all who are watching—even the ones I cannot see. In Jesus's name, amen.

Lesson 4

❊

Likewise Chosen

Read 1 Peter 5:12–14

No one writes their story alone. As Peter wrapped up his short letter, he acknowledged those who helped him lift his pen. First, Silvanus, who is also called Silas. Peter referred to Silvanus as his "faithful brother." Silvanus may have even helped Peter write this letter, as he helped Paul write several of his letters (see 2 Corinthians 1:19 and 1 and 2 Thessalonians 1:1). It's likely that Silvanus carried the letter to elect exiles in the five regions mentioned in Peter's greeting, read it aloud to them, and answered their questions. There was obviously synergy, trust, and rapport between the two men so that Peter could confidently place this difficult and important message into Silvanus's hands.

The elect exiles who received the letter were probably as dumbfounded as we have been to hear Peter's upside-down and inside-out commands. Rejoice in suffering, even though you're hurting? Submit to all authorities, even the ones you disagree with? Bless those who curse you, instead of taking your own revenge? Oh my! Thousands of years have passed, and these words are still as hard for us to hear as they were for the first Christians.

Mark is also mentioned fondly; Peter refers to him as a "son." Although the Gospel of Mark does not state its author, the early church unanimously believed it was written by this early follower of Jesus who traveled with Jesus and Peter as well as Paul. Peter provided much of the firsthand testimony for Mark's fast-paced and action-packed book about Jesus's ministry, miracles, and mission.

Peter also sends greetings from a third person:

> She who is at Babylon, who is likewise chosen, sends you greetings. (1 Peter 5:13)

Scholars have three opinions about who "she" could refer to in this verse. "She" could be a reference to the church in Rome—the church was referred to in the feminine, and Rome was a city as sinful as Babylon. This cryptic mention would help conceal their location and avoid widespread persecution in the region at that time. Or Peter may have been staying in the actual city of Babylon when he wrote this letter, which had a vibrant Jewish community at the time; "she" could be the church in Babylon. But I prefer the third opinion, which is that "she" could be a reference to Peter's wife, who accompanied him (see 1 Corinthians 9:5). Since this greeting is sandwiched between two real men, Silvanus and Mark, some biblical scholars believe it's likely that Peter was referring to a real woman.[3]

Jesus was surrounded by women from the cradle to the cross. Jesus ministered to women, and women ministered to Jesus (see Luke 8:1–3). Because Peter followed Jesus, he was also surrounded by these female followers of Jesus, as well as his wife, his mother-in-law, and possibly even a daughter of his own according to early tradition. Jesus demonstrated daily to Peter that women are equally esteemed in his kingdom, and we saw in Peter's own letter that he heeded these lessons well.

We won't know this side of heaven who Peter meant in this verse, but we do know that women are "likewise chosen" to be disciples of Jesus who hear his teaching, listen and understand, then follow and obey.

Like you.

God has "likewise chosen" you as purposefully as he chose Peter. He carefully picked out all your personality quirks and placed you in your community at this moment to serve his people as only you can. He knew each mistake you'd make along the way and set in motion a plan for your redemption before he hung the first star in the sky.

God has written you into his story, for his glory.

This. Changes. Everything!

You might think it's inappropriate and unlikely, if not impossible, to find joy on this arduous journey through the end of the world as you know it. You'll want to leave your TEOTWAWKI times behind.

You'll change your mind.

One day, you'll actually miss it. You'll long for the intimacy you had with Jesus when you were trembling in fear and he tenderly lifted you up. A candle that smells just like the hospital chapel will remind you where the Holy Spirit met you in your hour of deepest need. You won't be able to imagine what life was like before you met your best friend the day her bumpy path crossed yours.

There is a point to your pain if it points to Jesus. As you carry your trembling, cracked cup along the long road home through the pain, you'll fill it with more than hope and joy—you'll overflow it with power. You'll discover the heights of praise not possible until you've reached the depths of despair.

This paradigm shift turns suffering to worship. It brings our focus from what hurts us to how God heals us, from our pain to his purpose, from our agony to his glory. This is how to turn uncertain times into a surprisingly hopeful new normal.

Sweet friend, we don't need to fear the end of the world as we know it. Jesus wrote the end. Jesus is the end.

> "I am the Alpha and the Omega—the beginning and the end," says the Lord God. "I am the one who is, who always was, and who is still to come—the Almighty One." (Revelation 1:8 NLT)

The End

I'd like to end my book the way Peter ended his, with words of encouragement and comfort:

> My purpose in writing is to encourage you and assure you that what you are experiencing is truly part of God's grace for you. Stand firm in this grace. (1 Peter 5:12 NLT)

Whatever you may be experiencing—the loss, the shame, the pain—can be entrusted to God's hands. Stand firm in his grace. God's grace is unshakable when your world crumbles and unstoppable when your dreams come to an end. Yesterday's trials have prepared you for tomorrow's troubles. You are ready for whatever comes next.

> Peace to all of you who are in Christ. (1 Peter 5:14)

If you are "in Christ"—your past sins covered by his blood, your present suffering eased by his own, and your future secure in his promises—then you are at peace with God. Stand firm knowing you are capable, called, and equipped. Your mind is ready for action. His grace and glory are being revealed to you and reflected to untold onlookers. Your cup runneth over!

You've learned how to apply 1 Peter principles to life's pain. In 1 Peter 1, you made sense of suffering that can seem endless and pointless by synchronizing your heart with the ticking of God's eternal clock. In 1 Peter 2 you grasped God's purposes in choosing you for himself. You can now react to chaos and confusion with a calm, clearheaded response after reading 1 Peter 3's advice about Christlike conduct. Instead of being overwhelmed with emotion, you have a plan to express what you *feel*, identify what is *real*, and wisely determine how to *deal* with the situation. You did some intense soul renovation in 1 Peter 4, and the contrast between your old self and new self shines brightly! You have a toolbox full of five specific strategies you can control when you face the end of the world as you know it, the disappointing end of your own hopes, dreams, and desires. Your journey through these 105 verses concluded with 1 Peter 5 as you shed the shame of past mistakes and shared your compelling story for God's glory.

Hope fully, sweet friend.

. . . not on a cure.

. . . not on a relationship.

. . . not on a bank balance.

. . . not on a specific outcome.

. . . not on happy circumstances.

. . . not on anything but Jesus, always Jesus, only Jesus.

Jesus is the beginning, middle, and end of your story.

Hope fully in him.

A SECOND CUP

 The psalmist wrote, "My suffering was good for me, for it taught me to pay attention to your decrees" in Psalm 119:71 (NLT). How have you experienced this in your own life?

Re-create the following table in your journal and summarize what 1 Peter taught you about each theme:

Chapter	Theme	Symbol	Meaning
1	Clock	O	
2	Chosen	O	
3	Conduct	O	
4	Contrast	O	
5	Control	O	
6	Compel	O	

Dear heavenly Father, your clock is set for eternity, and I trust your unchanging character for heaven and the here and now. Thank you that I am chosen to be yours, just like Jesus. Please help me to conduct myself in a holy way, even during an unholy mess. May the contrast in my life now that I'm walking with you be obvious and apparent, so that others marvel at my Before-and-After life. When I'm facing the end of the world as I know it, I will survive using strategies that are always in my control. Compel others toward your kingdom as they see your glory in my story. I hope fully in Christ alone and stand firmly in my faith in you. In Jesus's great and precious name, amen.

Acknowledgments

MUCH LOVE AND MANY THANKS to—

David, who always encourages and never complains. Thanks for the grace, babe. I love you more, and I treasure the life we've crafted together.

Mom and Dad, whose prayers have sustained me since before I was born. You have walked worthy, and your children (and grandchildren!) are following. I thank God for you!

Bettie, Susan, Joe, Wendy, Christian, Brianna, and Carter for your constant prayers, group texts, funny memes, and daily Wordles that were just the right mix of motivation and distraction.

Ron and Marilyn, for feeding me and giving me a home (spiritually and literally) since our very first Friendiversary—and now we are neighbors forevermore.

ClearView Community Church in Colorado and the Women's Ministry Team for hosting this teaching, the women who shared their stories, and those who have prayed faithfully since the beginning like Sally and Debbie.

Seven Rivers Church in Florida for the writing space, inspiring sermons, and enriching friendships—and the staff at Seven Rivers Christian School for all those restroom breaks.

Jen Allee and my manuscript development team, who found every

ACKNOWLEDGMENTS

rough place and cheered as we smoothed them out. You've made this a better book for each reader, for God's glory!

My writerly friends Leslie, Peggy, Jessica, and Rachel for cross-country high fives, masterful critique, and conference sleepovers.

Blythe Daniel, my talented literary agent, and the team at Kregel Publications for believing this timeless message needed to be told today.

Michelle, Kelly, Jennifer, and Sarah for being so bold and brave. You make me love Jesus more, and I love each of you dearly.

And to Emma—my daughter, my friend. This one is for you, sweetheart. I love you.

Appendix

How to Share Your Story

Visit www.amylively.com/my-story or scan this code for a free template you can customize, save, and print.

Recognize
Identify a time in your life when you know the Lord was doing a mighty work in your heart. It may have been a problem or dilemma, a change, a time of suffering, a conflict, even a time of renewal or opportunity. It may be a whole season, or perhaps it's only one scene. You probably already have a title for this story in your head, like "That Time I Moved to Colorado" or "The Flat Tire."

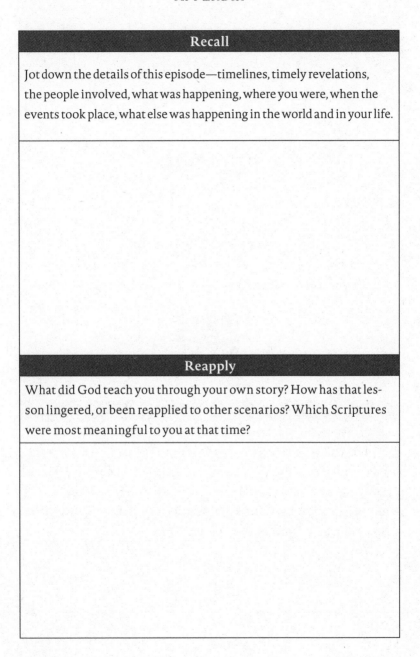

Recall

Jot down the details of this episode—timelines, timely revelations, the people involved, what was happening, where you were, when the events took place, what else was happening in the world and in your life.

Reapply

What did God teach you through your own story? How has that lesson lingered, or been reapplied to other scenarios? Which Scriptures were most meaningful to you at that time?

Release	
Give your story a little thought and a lot of prayer as you release it to the world.	
What to Leave In facts, feelings, blunders	**What to Leave Out** innocent, guilty, gory details, lewdness
When to Shut Up If you can check either of these boxes, it may not be time to release your story yet:	**When to Speak Up** If you can check either of these boxes, it may be time to release your story now:
☐ You are unable to share without bitterness, anger, or resentment. ☐ Your listener needs more sympathy and empathy as she takes time to process her own story.	☐ Your story points to the gospel story of God's redemption, grace, and mercy. ☐ Your listener desperately needs hope to hold on to as her own story unfolds.

Notes

Begin Here

1. Michael Card, *A Fragile Stone: The Emotional Life of Simon Peter* (Downers Grove, IL: InterVarsity Press, 2003), 12.

Chapter 1: Heaven and the Here and Now

1. Harper Douglas, "Etymology of Simon," Online Etymology Dictionary, accessed January 24, 2023, https://www.etymonline.com /word/Simon.

2. Blue Letter Bible, "Strong's G2786, *kephas*," accessed February 13, 2023, https://www.blueletterbible.org/lexicon/g2786.

3. Karen H. Jobes, *1 Peter*, Baker Exegetical Commentary on the New Testament (Grand Rapids, MI: Baker Academic, 2005), 26–30.

4. Tom Metcalfe, "Underground City Unearthed in Turkey May Have Been Refuge for Early Christians," Live Science, May 13, 2022, https://www.livescience.com/christians-hid-from-romans -in-underground-city.

5. Jobes, *1 Peter*, 1.

6. Larry R. Helyer, *The Life and Witness of Peter* (Downers Grove, IL: IVP Academic, 2012), 117.

7. Blue Letter Bible, "Strong's G5485, *charis*," accessed February 25, 2022, https://www.blueletterbible.org/lexicon/g5485.

8. *The Church History of Eusebius* III.30 in *A Select Library of Nicene and Post-Nicene Fathers of the Christian Church, Second Series* vol. 1, ed. Philip Schaff and Henry Wace (New York: The Christian Literature Company, 1890), 89.

Chapter 2: Just like Jesus

1. Chuck Bumgardner, "The Thickness of the Temple Veil," *Orchard Keeper* (blog), April 6, 2010, accessed March 7, 2022, https://cbumgardner.wordpress.com/2010/04/06/the-thickness -of-the-temple-veil.

2. Hayim Donin, *To Pray as a Jew: A Guide to the Prayer Book and the Synagogue Service* (New York: Basic Books, 1991), 68, 95.

3. F. K. Young, *Judaism for OCR Religious Studies GCSE (9–1)* (Peterborough, UK: Serpentine Green Books, 2016), 28–30.

4. A. W. Tozer, *The Pursuit of God* (Camp Hill, PA: Serenity, 1948), 46–47.

5. Tim Bartee, "May You Be Covered with the Dust of Your Rabbi," *Sidney Daily News*, October 19, 2016, https://www.sidneydai lynews.com/news/religion/48792/may-you-be-covered-with -the-dust-of-your-rabbi.

6. Charles Taylor, chap. 1 in *Sayings of the Jewish Fathers: Comprising Pirqe Aboth in Hebrew and English, with Notes and Excursuses* (Cambridge: Cambridge University Press, 1897), https:// www.sacred-texts.com/jud/sjf/sjf03.htm.

7. Karen H. Jobes, *1 Peter*, Baker Exegetical Commentary on the New Testament (Grand Rapids, MI: Baker Academic, 2005), 200.

8. WordReference English-Greek Dictionary, s.v. "*arravónas* (αρραβώνας)," accessed February 27, 2023, https://www.wordrefer ence.com/gren/αρραβώνας.

9. "Finally Wearing Our Wedding Bands! (Greek Traditions Vol. 1)," *WeddingWire*, October 28, 2017, https://www.wed

dingwire.com/wedding-forums/finally-wearing-our-wedding
-bands-greek-traditions-vol-1/fce324b1a0e1d7d4.html.

Chapter 3: How to Handle an Unholy Mess

1. Karen H. Jobes, *1 Peter*, Baker Exegetical Commentary on the New Testament (Grand Rapids, MI: Baker Academic, 2005), 183.
2. Gaius Suetonius Tranquillus, *The Lives of the Twelve Caesars*, ed. T. Forester, trans. Alexander Thomson (London: George Bell and Sons, 1890), 318.
3. Arthur S. Hunt and Campbell C. Edgar, trans., *Select Papyri, Volume II: Public Documents, Codes and Regulations, Edicts and Orders, Public Announcements, Reports of Meetings, Judicial Business, . . . and Others*, Loeb Classical Library 282 (Cambridge, MA: Harvard University Press, 1934), 78–89.
4. Hans-Josef Klauck, *Ancient Letters and the New Testament: A Guide to Context and Exegesis* (Waco, TX: Baylor University Press, 2006), 98.
5. *The Complete Works of Tacitus*, ed. Moses Hadas, trans. William Jackson Brodribb, The Modern Library (New York: Random House, 1942), 15.44, online at Perseus Digital Library, http://www.perseus.tufts.edu/hopper/text?doc=urn:cts:latinLit :phi1351.phi005.perseus-eng1:15.44.
6. Jobes, *1 Peter*, 185.
7. "Countries that Still Have Slavery 2023," World Population Review, accessed February 17, 2023, https://worldpopulationre view.com/country-rankings/countries-that-still-have-slavery.
8. "Slaves and Freemen," PBS, accessed March 14, 2022, https:// www.pbs.org/empires/romans/empire/slaves_freemen.html.
9. *Encyclopedia Britannica*, s.v. "American Anti-Slavery Society," accessed February 17, 2023, https://www.britannica.com/topic /American-Anti-Slavery-Society.

10. Tim Stafford, "The Abolitionists," *Christianity Today*, accessed February 17, 2023, https://www.christianitytoday.com/history /issues/issue-33/abolitionists.html.
11. *Plutarch's Moralia*, trans. Frank C. Babbitt, Loeb Classical Library 2 (Cambridge, MA: Harvard University Press, 1971), 311.
12. Jobes, *1 Peter*, 202.
13. Neel Burton, "The Battle of the Sexes," *Psychology Today*, July 2, 2012, https://www.psychologytoday.com/us/blog/hide-and-seek /201207/the-battle-the-sexes.

Chapter 4: Before and After

1. Paul Tripp, "A Psalm that Has No Hope," *Wednesday Word: A Weekly Devotional with Paul Tripp* (blog), June 30, 2021, https:// www.paultripp.com/wednesdays-word/posts/a-psalm-that-has -no-hope.

Chapter 5: How to Survive the End of the World

1. Jeanet Sinding Bentzen, "In Crisis, We Pray: Religiosity and the COVID-19 Pandemic," *Journal of Economic Behavior and Organization* 192 (2021): 541–83.
2. Roger T. Beckwith, *Calendar, Chronology, and Worship: Studies in Ancient Judaism and Early Christianity* (Leiden, Neth.: Brill, 2005), 193.
3. R. Herbert, "What Does the Biblical Word 'Abba' Really Mean?," *LivingWithFaith.org*, accessed April 7, 2022, http://www.living withfaith.org/what-does-abba-really-mean.html.
4. Heather Riggleman, "What Is the Meaning and Significance of Eros (God's Love) in the Bible?" Christianity.com, December 2, 2019, https://www.christianity.com/wiki/christian-terms/what-is -the-meaning-and-significance-of-eros-gods-love-in-the-bible .html.

5. Frederick W. Danker, *A Greek-English Lexicon of the New Testament and Other Early Christian Literature*, 3rd ed. (Chicago: University of Chicago Press, 2000), 6.

6. Jerome S. Hahn, *Bible Basics: An Introduction and Reference Guide to the Five Books of Moses* (Boca Raton, FL: International Traditions Corporation, 1996), 41, 45, 59.

7. Amy Lively, *How to Love Your Neighbor Without Being Weird* (Minneapolis, MN: Bethany House, 2015), 48.

8. Rajiv Tandon, "COVID-19 and Mental Health: Preserving Humanity, Maintaining Sanity, and Promoting Health," *Asian Journal of Psychiatry* 51 (June 20, 2020): https://www.ncbi.nlm.nih.gov/pmc/articles/PMC7305748/.

9. Randy Bressler, "Tell Me All I Need to Know About Oxytocin," Psycom.net, September 23, 2021, https://www.psycom.net/oxytocin.

10. Kelly McGonigal, "How to Transform Stress into Courage and Connection," Greater Good Science Center at the University of California, May 13, 2015, https://greatergood.berkeley.edu/article/item/how_to_transform_stress_courage_connection.

11. Blue Letter Bible, "Strong's G5382, *philoxenos*," accessed February 20, 2023, https://www.blueletterbible.org/lexicon/g5382.

12. Blue Letter Bible, "Strong's G5384, *philos*," accessed February 20, 2023, https://www.blueletterbible.org/lexicon/g5384.

13. Blue Letter Bible, "Strong's G3581, *xenos*," accessed February 20, 2023, https://www.blueletterbible.org/lexicon/g3581.

14. Michael Card, *A Fragile Stone: The Emotional Life of Simon Peter* (Downers Grove, IL: InterVarsity Press, 2003), 163.

15. J. P. Kirsch, "St. Peter, Prince of the Apostles," *The Catholic Encyclopedia*, accessed January 13, 2023, https://www.newadvent.org/cathen/11744a.htm.

NOTES

Chapter 6: Your Story for God's Glory

1. Steven J. Binz, *Saint Peter: Flawed, Forgiven, and Faithful* (Chicago: Loyola Press, 2015), 33.
2. Bobby Conway, *The Fifth Gospel: Matthew, Mark, Luke, John . . . You* (Eugene, OR: Harvest House, 2014), 9.
3. Marg Mowczko, "Who Is 'She' Who Is in Babylon? (1 Peter 5:13)," *Marg Mowczko* (blog), March 10, 2020, https://margmowczko.com/she-who-is-in-babylon-1-peter-513/.

About Amy

Amy Lively's passion is teaching God's Word as a "how-to manual" for loving him and loving others. Amy is a Bible teacher, speaker, and author of *How to Love Your Neighbor Without Being Weird.* She founded The Neighborhood Café, an international ministry helping women host neighborhood Bible studies in their homes. Amy has leadership experience in church planting, pastoring, women's ministry, small groups, and parachurch organizations. She is also a church volunteer, community organizer, and business owner. She and David, her husband of more than thirty years, have a grown daughter, Emma; they divide their time between Colorado and Florida with their holy dog and unsaintly cat. Connect with Amy at amylively.com.